The Forgotten Chapters

My Journey into the Past

Katherine Dimancescu

First Edition 2013

ISBN 978.0.9896169.0.4

Designed by Trish LaPointe, tslapointedesign.com

Set in Centaur type by Trish LaPointe.

Printed in the United States of America.

The cover image is "A Mapp of New England" (circa 1675) by John Seller. Map reproduction courtesy of the Norman B. Leventhal Map Center at the Boston Public Library, Boston, Massachusetts.

This book is dedicated to my brother Nick
(1985-2011)
"A True Knight of the Sky"

Contents

one

Discovering Denisons

In American history classes, I read chronicles of incredible individuals who possessed courage, passion, and visions that shaped the United States. Researching my ancestors who emigrated to America between 1620 and 1805 provided insights into the settlement of New England. Prominent ancestors who surfaced from the pages of history books included William and Mary Dyer, John and Priscilla Alden, Captain John Underhill, Captain George Denison, and Reverend Thomas Shepard. My recognition of my ancestors prompted me to share their stories that offer a personalized lens through which to take in our nation's history.

An eighth-grade family history research project initially inspired a passion for genealogy and the search for maternal ancestors. There were few forgotten chapters on my father's side of the family. His family roots in Romania going back to the late fifteen hundreds had been documented. His family had been prominent landowners, who owned property in Wallachia for centuries. My grandfather, D. D. Dimancescu, was a Romanian diplomat who fought in World War I on the side of the Allies. His diplomatic postings included San Francisco and later, England where he lived with his family during World War II. After the war ended, he attended the Paris Peace Conference in 1946. Less was known about my maternal ancestors. At first, mapping out my mother's family tree was a challenge. My curiosity was piqued by a family lineage establishing connections to Connecticut in the sixteen hundreds. This book is the

Author's Photo: Granite monument erected in memory of Captain George Denison and his second wife, Ann (Borodell) Denison. Ann's small headstone is to the right of the monument. Ann passed away at the age of 97 on September 26, 1712. Elm Grove Cemetery, Mystic, Connecticut.

story of what unfolded when I set out in search of my American ancestry. Piecing together the forgotten chapters of my family narrative was an experience that spanned nearly twenty years with primary research in both America and England.

Long after I finished my eighth-grade family history project, I continued to research my ancestors. My family roots unexpectedly became part of the discussion when I applied to college. In high school at my first meeting with the college counselor, I happily announced that I planned to apply for early decision to Bowdoin College in Maine. I had toured the school over the summer, spoken to alumni, and looked at courses and programs; I thought that Bowdoin was a perfect fit for me. There were, of course, practical considerations about attending a college in Maine: long dark icy New England winters and mud season (Maine's alternative version of spring). After hearing me express my enthusiasm for Bowdoin, the college counselor said in a calm tone, gleaned after years of advising students, "Well, if that is what you have decided, I am here to help you. I think it will be wise for you to also meet with representatives from other small liberal arts colleges."

I met with admissions officers, many of them representing colleges in the Midwest. In early December 1998, an admissions officer came from Denison University. To make this meeting on time, I left an honors history class early, and as I stepped outdoors onto the campus quad, the chilly dark afternoon reflected my mood. I did not want to hear about a college in Ohio because I had my mind set on attending a college on the East Coast.

As I climbed the stairs to the college office, I paused, struck by thoughts that Ohio had tornadoes, corn fields, and no ocean breezes, and it was very far away from home. During our meeting, the admissions officer talked about Denison University's history program and the town of Granville, which was settled by people from Massachusetts in the early eighteen hundreds. He said the town had an East Coast look with a touch of midwestern friendliness.

A few days later, a thin envelope arrived from Bowdoin College delivering unwelcome news. I had not been accepted for early decision. Now the waiting game began to see if I was accepted in the spring. In what I silently labeled as a "where-is-my-future-college-plan-headed" meeting with my patient college counselor, I sat there listlessly, my face red and puffy from crying. He said, "At this point, it makes sense for you to apply to other colleges. The college counselor from Denison

The Denison Homestead in Mystic, Connecticut. The larger house picture was taken by the author in August 2013. The smaller image of the homestead appeared in a 1903 publication, *The Homes of Our Ancestors in Stonington, Conn.* by Grace Denison Wheeler. The Denison Homestead and its parcel of 160 acres has been owned by the Denison family since Captain George settled in Mystic in 1654.

University said he would welcome your application. Another option could be Transylvania University in Kentucky. As I recall, your father's family is from Romania, specifically Transylvania, isn't it? Of course, you would be studying in Kentucky, not eastern Europe. With your last name and heritage, you could bring a lot to the college."

When college acceptance letters arrived in the mail, I was in the Australian rainforest on a school trip. This was an unlikely place to hear college acceptance news. When I located a pay phone and called home, my mother said quickly and happily on the other end, "Your first acceptance letter is here. It's from Denison University in Ohio." There was more good news. Denison was offering me a scholarship! I thought I could hear champagne corks popping at home as my parents celebrated this great news. Weeks later, a letter arrived from Bowdoin which stated I had not been accepted. Naturally, Denison became a top choice. Touring the campus in early May with trees in bloom, I fell in love with Denison University and decided to attend. I had no idea that I was

A photo taken during author's first visit to the Ancient Burying Ground in Hartford, Connecticut. The moment when the author first saw Captain George Denison's headstone was captured by her father, Dan Dimancescu. George was a member of the General Assembly in Connecticut. He passed away on October 23, 1694 while the assembly was in session in Hartford. He was buried in the Ancient Burying Ground not near his home in Mystic. George's current headstone replaced an earlier headstone, which can be seen at the Denison Homestead in Mystic, Connecticut. George's footstone (not pictured here) likely dates back to 1694.

about to become a Denison who attended Denison University.

When Denison University was first mentioned, I recalled the name "Denison" from my eighth-grade family history project. I discovered I had an ancestor named Captain George Denison, who lived in seventeeth-century Mystic, Connecticut. Ancestral connections between Captain George and William S. Denison, who was the benefactor of the university, did not cross my mind in eighth grade. Years later, I discovered William was a fellow descendant of Captain George.

In the years after I graduated from college, more Denison family connections came to light. I found ancient cemeteries where Denisons were laid to rest, family stories full of valor, warfare, love, and historic houses. I learned that George emigrated from Bishop's Stortford, England, with his parents, William and Margaret (Chandler) Denison, and two of his brothers, Daniel and Edward. They arrived in New England in November 1631 onboard the *Lyon* with Reverend John Eliot, who tutored George during the voyage from England. George and his family settled in Roxbury, Massachusetts. Reverend Eliot also settled in Roxbury, and a year later he started preaching in the newly established First Church in Roxbury. William became the third member and his wife, Margaret, the thirty-third member of this church.

The year 1632 was important for William and his family. His church membership paved the way for him to achieve the status of freeman on July 3, 1632[1]. Being a freeman in the Massachusetts Bay Colony was significant because "it gave one the right to vote for colony officers. In some colonies, though, freemanship was tied to church membership, and so the meaning was somewhat different. Massachusetts Bay and New Haven, the most Puritan of Puritan colonies, made church membership a prerequisite for freemanship, while the rest of the New England colonies did not."[2] On October 18, 1632, William's son, Daniel, married Patience Dudley, whose father, Thomas Dudley, became Governor of the Massachusetts Bay Colony. Patience's sister Anne (Dudley) Bradstreet is "considered by many to be the first American poet."[3]

By 1642, William was ranked as "one of the five wealthiest men in Roxbury," as he had a "personal estate of £24 7s. and real estate of seven acres valued at £6 8s."[4] He and Margaret celebrated the marriage of their son George and his first wife, Bridget Thompson, in March 1640, and then the marriage of their son Edward and his wife, Elizabeth Weld, the following year on March 30, 1641. The newlyweds all stayed in Roxbury, unlike Daniel and Patience who moved to Ipswich, Massachusetts, a few years after their marriage.

I discovered there are Denison cousins alive today around the world. Some Denison cousins use an alternate spelling of the name, Dennison, instead of Denison. One historic location, in particular, the Denison Homestead, links cousins who are descendants of Captain George Denison. It is a place that many of the family have found while researching our Denison roots in Mystic, Connecticut. We have stepped over its historic threshold to discover the homestead, built in 1717 by Captain George Denison who was named in honor of his paternal grandfather, Captain George.

Beholding the Denison Homestead for the first time made for a breathtaking sight. The homestead, the antique barn across the street, and the rolling meadow were a classic New England scene conjuring up the past. The meadow below the homestead was once a training ground for Captain George and his fellow soldiers as they prepared to fight during King Philip's War (1675–1676). The Denison Homestead, also known as Pequotsepos Manor, is now a house museum open to the public. Touring its rooms offered perspectives into Denison family history during different eras of America's history. The homestead sits in the midst of 160 acres, which were originally owned by Captain George, who settled here in 1654. There has been a Denison presence in this location for over 350 years. If Captain George returned to his former haunts, he would be pleased with how the Denison legacy has endured. Now the homestead is creating new opportunities to educate both Denison descendants and the public about colonial New England history by hosting historic reenactments, lectures, and other community events.

Burial site of John and Priscilla (Mullins) Alden, Standish Burial Grounds, Duxbury, Massachusetts. Photo taken by the author in November 2011.

"Why don't you speak for yourself, John?"

When I was in grade school in Massachusetts, each year as Thanksgiving approached, I was captivated by stories about the Pilgrims and their experiences after the *Mayflower* brought them to their new home in Plymouth, Massachusetts. One of my favorite tales concerned Priscilla Mullins, who was orphaned after the deaths of her parents, William and Alice, and her brother Joseph during their first year in Plymouth. William died during the difficult first winter in Plymouth. Sometime before November 1621, Alice and Joseph had also passed away. The knowledge that Priscilla was my maternal ancestor came to light much later. In the nineteenth century, her descendant, Henry Wadsworth Longfellow, penned a poem about Priscilla's courtship. My fascination with Priscilla was piqued when I first heard Longfellow's poem, "The Courtship of Miles Standish" read aloud in class. I closed my eyes and let my imagination conjure up romantic scenes of courtship in Plymouth as Captain Myles Standish and John Alden wooed Priscilla.

According to the Alden House Historic Site's Speak For Thyself Awards,

America's tradition of strong women began with the *Mayflower*. One of the best-loved examples in American history and literature is Priscilla Mullins (later Priscilla Alden). The great poet Henry Wadsworth Longfellow, himself a descendant of John Alden and Priscilla Mullins Alden, made their romance the center of his great

Photo of the author taken at the 113th Alden Kindred of America Annual Meeting, August 2013, Duxbury, Massachusetts. The Alden House (in the background) and its surrounding two and a half acres have always been owned by the Alden family.

epic "The Courtship of Miles Standish." He vividly imagined a scene in early Plymouth Colony. Two *Mayflower* passengers, the shy (and handsome) John Alden and the gruff and inarticulate Captain Miles Standish, have both fallen in love with the lovely Priscilla Mullins. The Captain beseeches John to approach Priscilla on his behalf. John, bound by friendship and duty, reluctantly agrees to set aside his own strong feelings. Priscilla, however, makes her own choice. She asks, in her own gracious, charming, modest, but absolutely determined way— "Why don't you speak for yourself, John?"[1]

The discovery that Priscilla was my ancestor made me curious about the woman Longfellow immortalized. Who was the real Priscilla Mullins? What was her life like after John spoke up and she accepted his proposal of marriage? In November 2010, with the Thanksgiving holiday on the horizon, my focus returned to John and Priscilla and their courtship. It was time for John and Priscilla to speak for themselves. The answers I sought about their married life and their legacies appeared in Duxbury, Massachusetts, at the Alden House Historic Site. Touring the house, walking around its grounds, and visiting the burial markers erected in memory of John and Priscilla brought chapters of their lives to light. If Priscilla had not encouraged John to speak for himself and she had married Captain Miles Standish, a very different history would have been recorded. The house, the grounds, and Alden family history spoke for themselves, and I learned by listening and observing.

The Alden House brought to light the chapters of their lives together after John spoke up and he married Priscilla. The couple first lived in Plymouth until they were granted land in 1627 in nearby Duxbury, Massachusetts. The Alden Kindred of America, who own and operate the house stated that, "The first house built and occupied by John and Priscilla was a long, narrow house with a field stone foundation and a root cellar under the west end. Archeological excavations made in 1960 by Roland Wells Robbins revealed the cellar stones and that the house was about 10 ½ feet in width and 38 feet in length (here the Aldens raised 10 children!). Its size would have been similar to a modern mobile home, although the Alden house would have had a loft or second floor."[2]

This early home where the Aldens raised their family no longer exists.

> It was located about 760 feet southeast…of the present Alden House. There were the 'ruins' of an old well visible on the property before 1840, but that location is now lost. This original site was well known and visited by interested people as early as the 18th century, such as Rev. Timothy Alden (to whom we are indebted for the earliest record of the 'Courtship' story in 1814). A number of bricks, a halberd head, and possibly other unrecorded artifacts were retrieved from the old Alden cellar hole in the 19th century. The site was first professionally excavated and documented by historical archaeologist Roland Wells Robbins in 1960.[3]

As I stepped out of my car, I got my first glimpse of the Alden House. I felt as if I had walked into a Norman Rockwell painting. The

JOHN ALDEN
b. 1599
d. 1687 — 1621 — PRISCILLA MULLINS
d. 1657

DAVID ALDEN
b. 1646
d. 1719 — 1670 — MARY SOUTHWORTH
b. 1650
d. 1717

PRISCILLA ALDEN
b. 1679 DUXBURY CT.
d. STONINGTON CT. — JAN 4 1699 DUXBURY CT. — SAMUEL CHESEBROUGH
b. FEB 14 1674 STONINGTON CT.
d. 1735 STONINGTON CT.

PRUDENCE CHESEBROUGH
b. FEB 28 1722 STONINGTON CT.
d. FEB 1799 GROTON CT. — FEB 27 1737 STONINGTON CT. — JOHN STANTON
b. SEPT 29 1714 STONINGTON CT.
d. NOV 16 1762 GROTON CT.

PRUDENCE STANTON FANNING
b. NOV 7 1754 LEDYARD CT.
d. SEPT 23 1825 LEDYARD CT. — 1778 GROTON CT. — WILLIAM WILLIAMS IX
b. FEB 17 1741 LEDYARD CT.
d. NOV 18 1814 LEDYARD CT.

ERASTUS WILLIAMS
b. SEPT 16 1785 LEDYARD CONN.
d. NOV 11 1847 LEDYARD CONN. — FEB 15 1818 STONINGTON CONN — NANCY (ANNA) HEWITT
b. JUNE 23 1793 STONINGTON CT.
d. MAR 6 1876 CLERMONT IA

PRUDENCE ANNA WILLIAMS
b. SEPT 16 1821 LEDYARD CONN.
d. DEC 5 1886 CLERMONT IOWA — OCT 25 1841 LEDYARD CT. — GUSTAVUS ADOLPHUS APPELMAN
b. FEB 23 1817 MYSTIC CONN
d. NOV 4 1893 ELKADER IOWA

ELIAS HEWITT APPELMAN
b. MAY 7 1852
d. MARCH 8 1929 — NOV 30 1877 ILLYRIA IOWA — MABEL STEWART
b. OCTOBER 17 1862
d. SEPTEMBER 1961

FRANZ ALLEN APPELMAN
b. MAY 27 1901
d. NOV 4 1967 — SEPT 14 1929 — JOYCE ERNESTINE HENDERSON
b. JAN 7 1909

Genealogical record reprinted with permission from the Appelman family. This record shows the line of descent from John Alden through Erastus Williams shared by the author and her Appelman cousins.

home had recently been reshingled, it was surrounded by the last patches of rich fall colors, and scattered fall leaves littered the ground in a variety of warm hues. A wonderful aroma like roasted chestnuts filled the crisp November air. I was now walking on grounds that had been owned by the Aldens since the 1620s. My visit to Duxbury in 2010 ocurred 390 years after the *Mayflower* brought my ancestors to their new home in New England.

After learning about the small size of John and Priscilla's first Duxbury home, the Alden house museum felt spacious. It was built in the seventeenth century by one of John and Priscilla's sons. "Taking all of the evidence into consideration—family lore, archaeology and dendrochronological dating—it would appear that the core of the present house was built by Jonathan Alden, probably before the death of his father John, perhaps around the time of his marriage in 1672 when he needed a home for his new family. We may have to relinquish the idea of Priscilla ever having lived in the existing Alden House, although it is certainly located upon the family property."[4] Even if Priscilla did not live in the present Alden House, I learned so much about my Alden ancestors during my visit that it was worth it to see where later generations of Aldens lived.

In the company of Matthew Vigneau, the administrative manager for The Alden Kindred of America, I toured the Alden house. As we walked through the home's historic rooms, Matthew discussed the Alden family down the generations as he pointed out objects of interest in each room. The tour progressed at a measured pace, which afforded me the time and space to take in architectural details in each room. Matthew gave me a rich and broad perspective of daily life for generations of Aldens.

The highlight of my visit came when Matthew and I were chatting in the Great Room, which is, "with the room above it, the oldest part of the house, dating to the last third of the seventeenth century. When new, these rooms were essentially the entire house, except for a lean-to shed where the eastern end of the kitchen is now. However, the only elements now visible that are from that early period are the long 'summer beam' which crosses the ceiling and the chimney girt into which it runs above the fireplace."[5] Matthew shared with me the wonderful story of a recent visit by a film crew documenting a Vermont man's discovery of his *Mayflower* ancestors, John and Priscilla Alden.

A few weeks ago, a former carpenter who lives in a tent outside of Richmond, VT, came to Duxbury to learn about his family. A trip that took him to the Alden Homestead...[Sean] Plasse, 35, was the subject of a television program produced out of Brigham Young University titled "The Generations Project." The program focuses on people who are at crossroads in their life, Matthew Vigneau, the administrative manager for the Alden Kindred, explained. The idea is that by examining their family history, they can come to a conclusion about what direction to go in, or perhaps gain the courage to move in the direction they already wanted to go. In Plasse's case, that journey found him standing in the field behind the Alden School, where John and Priscilla's first home stood, talking with Jim Baker, curator emeritus for the Alden Kindred of America, learning that he was a descendant of the most famous romance in early American history.[6]

Headstones for John and Priscilla (Mullins) Alden erected by the Alden Kindred of America in 1930. Author's photos taken in November 2011.

To be standing in the Great Room hearing about Sean's visit and what he learned about his Alden ancestors echoed so much of what my own genealogical discoveries have meant in my life. I later learned that Sean is a writer, whose book could help make a difference in the lives of children with dyslexia. "As Kendall Wilcox, producer of "The Generations Project," put it, "Sean has a calling in life to do something out of the ordinary." Or as Plasse puts it, "I'm always going out on these quests." His current quest may have started when he decided to become a bone marrow donor for a woman he didn't know. Unfortunately, the procedure damaged his hips, making him unable to practice his trade as a carpenter. Plasse, who has struggled with dyslexia, decided to write a children's book, *The Brothers Plad*, whose protagonist also has the condition."[7] Reading about Sean's journey and why he chose to write a children's book made me proud to share Alden ancestry with him. Jim Baker, curator emeritus for the Alden Kindred of America, told Sean that John was "a cooper, who had been hired to maintain the barrels aboard the *Mayflower*. Rather than return home with the ship, he stayed behind, marrying Priscilla Mullins and gaining a status that he would have never gained had he returned to England."[8] What resonated with Sean after he heard about John's life was "that ability to reinvent himself in the New World."[9]

Touring the Alden House in the off season gave me the opportunity to ask questions and to enjoy time to contemplate my own Alden heritage. "Today, the Alden House, with its two and a half acres of land, has the distinction of being [in] the unique instance of still belonging to the same family to which it was originally issued in the land division of 1627."[10]

John and Priscilla had ten children. In spite of all the illnesses, trials, and tribulations that were an inherent part of colonial American life, eight of their children survived into adulthood and married. The Aldens had "69 grandchildren and nearly 500 great-grandchildren."[11] The number of Alden descendants alive today around the world is growing all the time.

My ancestor, David, was John and Priscilla's tenth child and youngest son. He was "a prominent member of the church, a man of great responsibility, and much employed in public business."[12] Learning that David was the youngest child was significant information for my family tree. If he was never born or had died before he married and had children of his own, I would not be here today.

By the mid-1670s, my maternal ancestors David and Mary

(Southworth) Alden were raising a family of six children in Duxbury. Their daughter, Priscilla Alden, whom they named in honor of her famous grandmother, moved to Connecticut after her marriage to Samuel Chesebrough. Thus it came to pass that less than one hundred years after the *Mayflower*'s landing that this branch of my family with its Alden heritage was established in Connecticut.

When I was researching Priscilla Alden's marriage to Samuel Chesebrough, a story surfaced that reminded me of the romantic stories of her grandmother Priscilla's courtship. "An unconfirmed story claimed, 'In 1698 Samuel Chesebro was attacked by robbers while in Duxbury, MA. His arm was broken defending himself, and Priscilla Alden nursed him, married him, and rode to Stonington behind him on a pillion, holding his broken arm' (*Alden Dau*)."[13] Given the fact that Priscilla was named in honor of her paternal grandmother, Priscilla Mullins, whose courtship Henry Wadsworth Longfellow glorified, it would be fitting that young Priscilla would have her own courtship story.

What enriches the extended Alden family circle in the twenty-first century is that each of John and Priscilla's descendants, myself included, speak for ourselves by leading lives of our own, and then we come together at Alden family reunions to rejoice in our shared heritage. My Alden ancestors were my earliest immigrant ancestors to meet, marry, and start a family in North America. John and Priscilla are the couple at the beginning of my maternal ancestral line in New England. I am a twelfth-generation descendant of theirs.

My curiosity about the final resting places of John and Priscilla (Mullins) Alden was first piqued when I visited the Alden House Historic Site. Before this visit, I spent the majority of my time researching family lines in Connecticut, Ohio, and Rhode Island. This genealogical research affirmed my descent from *Mayflower* passengers John and Priscilla Alden.

On Thanksgiving weekend 2011, I visited the Standish Cemetery in Duxbury, where John and Priscilla were laid to rest. By finding this particular burial ground, my journey to trace my roots in early colonial America was going back to its earliest origins, the *Mayflower* and its passengers. An Alden Kindred of America publication drew attention to unknown facts about Priscilla's death and both her and John's burial in this cemetery. "We do not know when Priscilla died…Although John and Priscilla are certainly buried in the churchyard at Duxbury, the original grave markers (which were probably made of wood) have long ago disappeared. The present stones in the cemetery, erected by the Alden Kindred in John and Priscilla's memory, are only placed in rough approximation of the gravesites."[14]

Matthew Vigneau was once again incredibly helpful with this genealogical research trip. As I drove to Duxbury to find the cemetery, a phrase from Matthew's email rolled around my mind, "I am always interested in the Standish Burial Ground as it contains an important part not only of the Alden story, but America's story as well." Matthew's sentiment echoed the essence of what my genealogical research was about. Through the process of discovering my maternal ancestry starting with the arrival of the *Mayflower*, I was also learning about the settlement of New England and early colonial American history.

My visit to the Standish Burial Ground took place on an especially warm day for November. This was one of the most accessible historic burial grounds that I have visited. Markers and signs indicated graves and memorials of interest. It was easy to locate the headstones erected to the memory of John and Priscilla in 1930 by the Alden Kindred of America. As a light breeze rustled the leaves of the surrounding trees, I knelt before their headstones and thought about how 391 years ago, a world away in England, these two individuals and their fellow *Mayflower* passengers had bravely embarked on a journey to start anew in a strange land.

What occurred to me was that John and Priscilla had shaped the earliest part of my family tree in America. Their lives, their choices, their heartaches, their sacrifices, their love, their endurance, and their joys had led to my visit to this cemetery almost four hundred years after the *Mayflower* landed.

THE
BOOK OF THE GENERAL

LAUUES AND LIBERTYES

CONCERNING THE INHABITANTS OF THE MASSACHUSETS
COLLECTED OUT OF THE RECORDS OF THE GENERAL COURT
FOR THE SEVERAL YEARS WHERIN THEY WERE MADE
AND ESTABLISHED,

And now revised by the same Court and disposed into an Alphabetical order
and published by the same Authorit.e in the General Court
held at *Boston* the fourteenth of the
first month *Anno*
1647.

Whosoever therefore resisteth the power, resisteth the ordinance of God,
and they that resist receive to themselves damnation. Romanes 13. 2.

CAMBRIDGE.
Printed according to order of the GENERAL COURT.
1648.

And are to be solde at the shop of *Hezekiah Usher*
in *Boston*

CHAPTER
three

Colonial Crimes and Punishments

T hree decades before the persecution of Quakers in the Massachusetts Bay Colony, Puritan authorities publicly reprimanded my ancestors Robert Coles and Walter Palmer for their actions. Robert was punished for being a drunkard, and Walter was put on trial for manslaughter. Walter emigrated from England with his family in 1629, and after disembarking in Salem, Massachusetts, he made his way to Charlestown, where he chose to reside. Robert left England in 1630, and he settled nearby in Roxbury. Both men arrived in New England during a period of huge immigration into the region. "Between 1620 and 1640…about twenty thousand English men, women, and children crossed the Atlantic to settle New England."[1] The landing of the *Mayflower* in 1620 brought the first wave of immigrants, and immigration did not slow down until the start of the English Civil War in the early 1640s. In the midst of the intense influx of individuals settling New England, the actions of these men put them in the public eye when they were held accountable for their behavior.

Cover page of *The Book of the General Lawes and Libertyes concerning the Inhabitants of the Massachusets* (1648). These laws were published in 1648 by the orders of the Massachusetts General Court and copies were made available in Hezekiah Usher's bookshop in Boston. Source: *Laws and Liberties of Massachusetts: Reprinted from the Unique Copy of the 1648 Edition in the Henry E. Huntington Library,* copyright 1998 by the Henry E. Huntington Library and Art Gallery, San Marino, California.

Excerpt from "Capital Lawes" section of The Book of the General Lawes and Libertyes concerning the Inhabitants of the Massachusets:

4. If any person shall commit any wilfull MURTHER, which is Man slaughter, committed upon premediate malice, hatred, or crueltie not in a mans necessary and just defence, nor by meer casualty against his will, he shall be put to death. Exod. 21. 12. 13. Numb. 35. 31

5. If any person flayeth another suddenly in his ANGER, or CRUELTY of passion, he shall be put to death. Levit. 24. 17. Numb. 35. 20. 21.

Source: *Laws and Liberties of Massachusetts: Reprinted from the Unique Copy of the 1648 Edition in the Henry E. Huntington Library,* copyright 1998 by the Henry E. Huntington Library and Art Gallery, San Marino, California.

      Robert became an active member of the Roxbury community. He established himself in his new home by becoming "member #8"[2] along with his first wife, Mary, who was "member # 34"[3] of the First Church in Roxbury; he became a freeman on May 18, 1631 and served as a representative to the General Court on May 9, 1632.[4] Restless, Robert uprooted his family and moved them first to Ipswich in 1633 and then to Salem in 1635. By 1635, Robert and Mary had become the parents of three children, John, Deliverance, and Ann (my ancestor).

      Unfortunately, there was more to Robert's life than just his roles as husband, father, and active member of the communities he called home in the 1630s. This was an age when Robert and his fellow colonists feared that drinking water would make them ill. The preferred liquid refreshments of the period were beer or wine, and these spirits got Robert into a great deal of trouble.

> The most difficult social problem to manage in colonial times was the widespread abuse of alcohol. Excessive drinking not only harmed the drinker but imposed heavy costs on society in the form of impoverished families and destitute children. The problem was complicated by the fact that total prohibition was out of the question. Social drinking had broad popular support as well as the approval of Scripture. Besides, alcohol was safer to drink than ordinary water, which in colonial times often contained lethal bacteria. Water mixed with a little alcohol was much safer than untreated water. The danger to health posed by the latter made wine and beer essential household items. So despite its potential for abuse, alcohol came close to being a universal beverage.[5]

I wondered what had made Robert a target for punishment for drunkenness in a society where consumption of alcohol was the norm. "The heart of the problem was that excessive drinking could not be quantified. An amount of alcohol sufficient to make one drinker drunk might have no effect on another. So the regulations had to target the effect on the drinker rather than the quantity consumed. Massachusetts made it unlawful for the drinker to become 'disabled in the use of his understanding,' a definition loose enough to cover everything from slight to total intoxication."[6] It was hard for me to gauge how intoxicated Robert was on the occasions for which he was fined.

> On 16 August 1631 [Robert was] fined five marks for being disorderly with drink. On 6 March 1631/2 "Rob[er]te Coles of Rocksbury," was fined 20s. for being drunk at Charlton in October last," and on 3 April 1632 he confessed his fault in attempting to excuse himself at the previous court, and had his fine remitted. On 3 September 1633 Robert Coles was fined £10 for "abusing himself shamefully with drink, enticing John Shotswell [and] his wife to incontinency, & other misdemeanor."

On 4 March 1634/5 it was ordered that Robert Coles "shall not pay more of his fine of £10, for drunkenness, &c, than hath been already levied in strong water." All of these fines were remitted or discharged in the general amnesty of 6 September 1638.[7]

Robert's fines for "being disorderly with drink" did not prohibit him from serving as a representative from Roxbury to the General Court in May 1632. After fining Robert repeatedly, the General Court ordered him to wear a letter similar to what Hester Prynne, the main character in Nathaniel Hawthorne's book, *The Scarlet Letter*, endured as her punishment. The decision to publicly shame Robert for his drinking problem was simple. "The courts sometimes tried to shame drunkards into sobriety. New Plymouth published lists of excessive drinkers to put taverns on notice and to pressure those listed to mend their ways or suffer a loss of social standing. In Massachusetts, the courts sometimes sentenced drunkards to wear identifying signs and symbols."[8]

On 4 March 1633/4 the General Court ordered that Robert Coles "for drunkenness by him committed at Rocksbury, shall be disfranchised, wear about his neck, & so to hang upon his outward garment a *D*, made of red cloth, & set upon white; to continue this for a year, & not to leave it off at any time when he comes amongst company, under penalty of 40s. for the first offense, & £5 the second, & after to be punished by the Court as they think meet; also, he is to wear the *D* outwards, & is enjoined to appear at the next General Court, & to continue there till the Court be ended." On 14 May 1634 the General Court ordered that the "sentence of Court inflicted upon Rob[er]te Coles, March 4th, 1633, for drunkenness, &c, by him committed, is now reversed, upon his submission, & testimony being given of his good behavior."[9]

In an era centuries before the Internet, television, and social media outlets like Facebook, Robert's punishments served as a public-service message to the Roxbury community to show what fate awaited drunkards.

His drinking did impact other parts of his life, including his marriage. His church membership was revoked, and he was excommunicated. His position as a freeman was also impacted as he was "disenfranchised 4 March 1633/34, but apparently readmitted 14 May 1634."[10] Robert's readmission as a freeman was a result of his sobriety, which the General Court noted.[11] Robert was not the only Massachusetts Bay Colony resident publicly shamed for drunkenness. "In 1636 the Assistants Court ordered William Perkins to stand for an hour in public with "a white sheet of paper on his breast having a great D upon it."[12]

An esteemed member of the Roxbury community, Reverend John Eliot noted Robert's drunkenness and its impact on his first wife Mary. "Eliot note[d] that 'God also wrought upon her heart (as it was hoped) after her coming to N.E., but after her husband's excommunication & falls she did too much favor his ways, yet not as to incur any just blame, she lived an afflicted life, by reason of his unsettledness & removing from place to place;' she died by about 1637."[13] Sadly, Mary's life as Robert's wife and mother of their three children was difficult due to his drinking issues and frequent moves around the Massachusetts Bay Colony in her last years.

After his first wife's passing, Robert made big changes in his life. He married his second wife Mary Hawkshurst with whom he had four more children. He decided to leave Salem, his third place of residence in less than ten years. He chose to follow in the footsteps of Roger Williams, who had been a fellow resident of Salem and who was also persecuted by the Massachusetts Bay Colony. After his banishment from the Massachusetts Bay Colony in 1636, Roger Williams established the settlement of Providence, Rhode Island. In 1638, Robert uprooted his family again, moving them from Salem to Providence. Robert's wanderlust faded after he moved to Providence, where he lived from 1638 until 1653, when he moved to Warwick, Rhode Island. Robert successfully established himself in Providence—"he paid a town rate at Providence on 2 September 1650 totalling £3 6s. 8d., placing him among the five richest men in town."[14] By the time of his death in 1655, Robert had a great deal to be proud of, having overcome the stigma of public humiliation and punishment in the Massachusetts Bay Colony.

In the fall of 1630, the future of Walter Palmer and his five children hung precariously in the balance. Walter was facing manslaughter charges in the Massachusetts Bay Colony, being held solely responsible for the death of Austin Bratcher, who was "presumably one of the servants sent over in 1629 or 1630 by Matthew Craddock to work on his farm on the Mystic River."[15] Walter was still a relative newcomer to the Charlestown area, having arrived from England a year earlier. Walter was forty-five years old, and at around 6 feet 4 inches tall, he towered over his neighbors.

On September 28, 1630, "fifteen members of the coroner's jury, inhabitants of Boston, Charlestown, Dorchester, Roxbury, Salem, and Watertown"[16] came together to deliberate. The situation did not look good for Walter when the coroner's jury stated their verdict that, "We find that the strokes given by Walter Palmer were occasionally the means of death of Austen Bratcher, & so to be manslaughter."[17] Walter's family was lucky that he was not put in prison to await his trial; he was able to "put up bond of £40, with Ralph Sprague and John Stricklett [Strickland] as bondsmen, promising that Palmer would appear at the court of 19 October next, to answer for the death of Austen Bratcher."[18]

Given his impressive stature, Walter towered over members of the court, who assembled on October 19, 1630, when he made his scheduled appearance. No record referred to Walter being put in prison after making his court appearance, and presumably he went home to his residence in Charlestown to await the court's final verdict.

Less than a month after Walter appeared in court, on November 9, 1630, before a trial jury of twelve men: "Mr. Edmond Lockwood, Rich Morris, Willm Rockewell, Willm Balston, Christopher Conant, Willm Cheesebrough, Willm Phelpes, John Page, Willm Gallard, John Balshe, John Hoskins, and Laurence Leach."[19] One trial juror's name, William Chesebrough, stood out in the list, as he is also my ancestor. William's participation meant that this trial now involved two of my ancestors. Earlier in 1630, William had emigrated from England to Boston with his wife Anna and their children. William and Walter may have crossed paths soon after William's arrival, or perhaps they connected after the trial was over. William became a lifelong friend of Walter, a fellow founder of the town of Stonington, Connecticut, and before too long their families became strongly connected through marriages and children.

The jurors traveled from their homes in Boston, Dorchester, Salem, and Watertown,[20] and after spending time deliberating, "The jury findes Walter Palmer not quilty of manslaughter, whereof hee stoode indicted, & soe the court acquitts him."[21] Walter was a free man. The manslaughter charges and subsequent trial in no way affected his reputation in the Charlestown community, and afterward he "became very prominent in the affairs of Charlestown, holding public office and is listed among the first group of men who took the Oath of Freemen on May 18, 1631. The original list included, Mr. Roger Conant, John Balche, Ralfe Sprage, Simon Hoyte, Rick Sprage, Walt (Walter) Palmer, Abraham Palmer, Mr Rich Saltonstall, Rich Stower, Czekiell Richardson, Wm Cheesebrough."[22] Walter and his family managed to weather the precarious months in the fall of 1630 when the trial took place and his fate was unknown. As indication that he did not lose the respect of his fellow residents of Charlestown after his trial, "In 1635 Walter was elected a Selectman of Charlestown, and in 1636 Constable."[23] In June 1633, Walter married his second wife, Rebecca Short, in the First Church in Roxbury. Together they became parents to seven children of their own and parents to Walter's five children from his first marriage.

My ancestors, Robert Coles and Walter Palmer, immigrated to the Massachusetts Bay Colony when it was in its infancy. The ways in which they were disciplined showcased to their fellow citizens how authorities in this new colony handled deviant or criminal behavior. Robert's fines and the *D* he was forced to wear, coupled with Walter's summons to court to face manslaughter charges, were reminders to both these men, their families, and other residents of the colony that the authorities were not going to turn a blind eye to misdemeanors and other crimes. Robert and Walter did not let their retributions define the lives they were creating for themselves and their families in New England or their reputations, and they both eventually established new homes beyond the borders of the Massachusetts Bay Colony.

Author's March 2013 photo of the bronze statue of Mary Dyer on the west lawn of the Massachusetts State House, Boston, Massachusetts.

Quakers in New England

C ountless times I have walked past the bronze statue of
Mary Dyer, whose bronze figure gazes upon busy Beacon
Street and Boston Common. Her statue stands in front of
the Massachusetts State House in close proximity to busy
Beacon Street. Ancestral connections to Mary inspired
one of her descendants to set aside funds for this tribute: "Three
centuries after Mary Dyer's martyrdom, a descendant left a bequest that
paid for Sylvia Shaw Judson, a Quaker woman herself, to produce a life-
size bronze statue of Mary Dyer. In 1959 the statue was erected on the
west lawn of the Massachusetts State House, where it stands today."[1]

Mary's life story took on a new significance when I learned she
was my maternal ancestor. Mary was a Quaker martyr who was executed
in 1660 for her religious beliefs and for supporting fellow Quakers,
whom the Puritan authorities were persecuting. Mary's life story was
intriguing because the persecution of Quakers was little discussed in
history classes or in general conversations about the history of the
Commonwealth of Massachusetts. How could a wife and mother of six
children be hanged for the crime of being a Quaker? The answers I
uncovered revealed a disturbing chapter in Massachusetts history and
also revealed Mary's deep religious convictions.

While pregnant, Mary emigrated with her husband William
from London to Boston in 1635. By that December, the couple become
members of the First Church of Boston. It was in this congregational
church that their son Samuel was baptized soon after his birth. Being a
member of the church was important, for it allowed the members'
children to be baptized, and it also made men eligible to be freemen in

Author's March 2011 photo of St. Martin-in-the-Fields Church, London, England where Mary Barrett and William Dyer were married on October 27, 1633.

the colony. March 3, 1636, was a proud day for William when he officially became a freeman. "The Freemen were the only colonists who were franchised to vote, and the franchise was not offered to all. One generally had to be a mature male church-member, and must have experienced a transforming spiritual experience by God's grace, as attested by himself and confirmed by church leaders."[2] When William became a freeman, he was fortunate to be able to take an updated oath. There were many reticent male church members in Boston who did not agree with an earlier version of the oath and did not become freemen in the early 1630s.

> ...apparently, a number of qualifying church-members would not take the oath because they had problems with the wording. An oath in those times was taken very seriously, as though it were a promise made directly to the Almighty with one's soul forfeit in the breach. Numerous persons who are on church and court records of 1630–1632 did not take the oath until 1634, when the oath was shortened and modified to replace the persons of the Governor, etc., to whom obedience was due with the impersonal "common weale." Others, such as those who later became Quakers, objected strongly to oaths in general.[3]

By the end of 1636, William and Mary had achieved many life milestones during their first year in their new home. They had a healthy son Samuel and a home in Boston on Summer Street;[4] they were members of the First Church of Boston, and William was a freeman. This period of peacefulness in their lives was brief. In 1637, William and Mary supported their friend Anne Hutchinson during the Antinomian Controversy, and Mary gave birth to a stillborn baby. These two events altered the course of their lives forever.

> The term "antinomian" literally means "one who is against the law" (anti = against, nomos = the law) and was used by the orthodox Puritans as a slanderous term against Anne Hutchinson's followers. The main theological dispute between the antinomians and the orthodox Puritans revolved around the question of sanctification. As good Calvinists, the Puritans believed in predestination—that a person was chosen at birth either to receive God's grace of eternal life or to suffer the fiery torment of the pit. Grace was a gift from God that could not be earned by good works on earth. This idea was termed the "covenant of grace" and stood in contrast to a theory, not held by Puritans, that God's grace could be earned through good actions. This was called the "covenant of works." According to

the Puritans, a person could never really know for sure if he or she were among God's elect. Such doubt could lead to severe psychological problems for the intensely religious, but even more important, some way had to be found to differentiate between those who were saved ("justified") and those who were damned, since the Puritan church was based on the idea that only the saved could be true church members and take communion. Working on the theory that only the elect could lead a saintly life, the Puritans accepted outward appearance and action as criteria for acceptance into church membership ("sanctification"). Most Puritan ministers were quick to point out that though sanctification was based on earthly works, these works could not earn salvation.[5]

The beliefs and views espoused by Anne Hutchinson and shared by her supporters, including her brother-in-law Reverend John Wheelwright, were extremely threatening to Puritan authorities and religious leaders in Boston. The menace lay in the fact that "Hutchinson and her followers believed that until a person had had a direct religious experience with God, he or she could not know if they were saved. Thus, for Hutchinson, an inner experience replaced the outward appearance used by Puritan ministers to judge the saintliness of their flocks. One ramification directly followed from Hutchinson's position. If a person knew he or she were saved, then outward appearance and conformity with laws were not necessary. Hence the term 'antinomian.' "[6]

Anne Hutchinson was put on trial in 1637 and forced to answer questions posed by leading men in Boston, such as Governor John Winthrop. She delivered sharp answers as she was a educated woman who knew the Bible well. As for her brother-in-law Reverend Wheelwright, he got himself into trouble for the sermon he delivered on January 19, 1637. That particular day had been designated

A day of general fasting, to pray for God's healing for the "dissensions in our churches." The Bay Colony leaders had invited John Wheelwright to preach the fast-day sermon in the Boston church. The strategy produced anything but healing. Indeed, Wheelwright's sermon, which clearly reflected the leanings of the Hutchinson faction, produced a violent reaction within the community. By March, in fact, the General Court

One of four bronze tablets on the base of the monument erected in honor of Captain John Underhill. The white granite monument and obelisk were dedicated in a ceremony in the Underhill Burying Ground in Locust Valley, Long Island on July 11, 1908. President Theodore Roosevelt spoke at the dedication ceremony. The Underhill Burying Ground was established by Captain John Underhill, who was buried there in 1672. The monument and obelisk were placed upon the original burial site of Captain John and atop the obelisk is a bronze ball with a bronze eagle perched upon it. Author's photo taken in August 2012.

(although itself divided) had found it necessary to bring Wheelwright to trial. After deliberation, it found him guilty of "contempt" and "sedition." The Court's action did not go unnoticed. A "remonstrance," protesting Wheelwright's conviction, was circulated among the members of the Boston church (sixty signatures were collected) and then presented to the General Court.[7]

This was the first of two remonstrances signed by ancestors of mine to protest religious persecutions. One of the signers of the second remonstrance drafted twenty years later in Flushing, New Netherland, was Henry Townsend.

Original document bearing the signatures of Mary and William Dyer. Image courtesy of the Newport Historical Society, Newport, Rhode Island.

One of the signers of this first "remonstrance" submitted to support Wheelwright was my ancestor, Captain John Underhill. Boston authorities made sure he was disarmed due to his "liberal views,"[8] and "with his love of justice [had] signed a petition in his behalf [Reverend John Wheelwright] and in consequence [Underhill] was discharged from further service"[9] to the colony. John was punished for his support of Wheelwright along with other men in the Massachusetts Bay Colony, and on November 15, 1637,

> a number of men who had signed a petition in support of
> Wheelwright were disfranchised (that is, were stripped of their
> freemanship). On the 20th a larger number, mostly from Boston
> but some from a handful of other Massachusetts Bay towns,
> were disarmed as well. Within a few days, many of those named
> in the court records on the 15th and the 20th signed a petition
> in which they submitted to authority, stating that, "having
> joined in preferring to the Court a writing called a Remonstrance,
> or Petition, I acknowledge it was ill done,…and therefore I
> desire my name may be put out of it."[10]

By the end of 1637, Captain John Underhill was in London, where his account of The Pequot War titled *Newes From America* was published. John was not one of the men who "submitted to authority" and signed a petition recanting their support of Wheelwright. John firmly held his position that his religious beliefs were acceptable.[11] He was banished from the Massachusetts Bay Colony in 1638. He journeyed to present-day Exeter, New Hampshire, where Reverend Wheelwright had established a new home; John resided there for a year.

Another ancestor punished for supporting Anne Hutchinson and Reverend John Wheelwright during the Antinomian Controversy was William Denison, who was the father of Captain George Denison. On November 20, 1637, William Denison and his son Edward Denison were among a group of men from Roxbury who were disarmed for their support of Hutchinson and Wheelwright: "The magistrates also ordered that all signers of a petition protesting Wheelwright's banishment hand over their 'guns, pistols, swords, powder, shot, and match.'"[12]

As Anne Hutchinson's life in Boston tumbled down around her during the Antinomian Controversy, so did the lives of her good friends,

Mary and William Dyer. With assistance from Anne and another midwife, Jane Hawkins, Mary gave birth to a stillborn baby. The infant was quietly buried by Anne, Jane, and John Cotton, a friend of Anne's, with no notice of the stillbirth given to the authorities as was required by law. When this cover-up was discovered months later, Governor John Winthrop had the remains of the stillborn infant exhumed and carefully inspected. The infant was declared a monster. " 'Monster' was a term commonly used for more than a hundred years in England, to include conjoined twins, congenital birth defects, stillborn malformed babies, and even deformed living children."[13] Anne Hutchinson, her family, and the Dyers soon moved to Rhode Island. They worked hard to establish new lives for themselves in a setting far removed from the condemnation of Massachusetts Bay Colony authorities.

Mary and William Dyer's distress over the investigation into the burial of their stillborn child did not fully go away after they moved to Rhode Island. During a period of celebration for Mary's safe deliveries of healthy babies, the horrible news came to light that stories about her stillborn infant were being published overseas.

In 1642 and 1644, Massachusetts Governor John Winthrop's account of Mary Dyer's 1637 stillborn baby's deformation was published in England with a forward by Rev. Thomas Welde, one of Winthrop's colleagues. In *A Short Story of the Rise, Reign, and Ruin of the Antinomians, Familists, and Libertines That Infected the Churches of New England*, Winthrop's text described Mary's daughter: "It was of ordinary bigness; it had a face, but no head, and the ears stood upon the shoulders and were like an ape's; it had no forehead, but over the eyes four horns, hard and sharp; two of them were above one inch long, the other two shorter; the eyes standing out, and the mouth also; the nose hooked upward; all over the breast and back full of sharp pricks and scales, like a thornback [i.e., a skate or ray], the navel and all the belly, with the distinction of the sex, were where the back should be, and the back and hips before, where the belly should have been; behind, between the shoulders, it had two mouths, and in each of them a piece of red flesh sticking out; it had arms and legs as other children; but, instead of toes, it had on each foot three claws, like a young fowl, with sharp talons."[14]

Tragically, Anne Hutchinson did not enjoy a peaceful life for long after moving to Rhode Island. After the death of her husband, she chose to relocate with some members of her family to Long Island and then to present-day Pelham Bay, New York. In 1643, Native Americans, mistaking her for a Dutch settler, massacred Anne at her home along with members of her family and servants. The Native Americans had been attacking Dutch colonists living in the colony of New Netherland. Anne was survived by some of her children, who were not with her at the time of the massacre. Her daughter Susannah was out picking berries near their home. When the attack happened, she hid in a nearby cave but was discovered. The Native Americans considered this cave sacred and therefore spared her life, taking her captive. The Friends of Anne Hutchinson website shared the following additional information about Anne's death. "Anne Hutchinson's death was the result of conflicting land claims between the Dutch under Governor Kieft and local Siwanoys. Because of Kieft's brutality to the Natives, Anne, who practiced racial tolerance and refused to keep firearms, and all but the daughter Suzannah were brutally murdered in a retaliatory attack in August. 1643."[15] The tragic death of Anne Hutchinson was hard for Mary Dyer, as they were close friends who had supported each other through the most trying of times.

The 1640s were a time when Mary's focus was on her family and their farm in Newport, Rhode Island. After the birth of their last child in 1650, Mary and William visited England, and only William returned home to their farm and to their children. "In 1652 William and Mary Dyer accompanied Roger Williams and John Clarke on a political mission to England. Mary Dyer remained there five years, becoming a follower of George Fox, founder of the Society of Friends, whose doctrine of the Inner Light was not unlike Mrs. Hutchinson's 'Antinomianism.' "[16] It had been seventeen years since William and Mary left England bound for Boston, and now they were returning to England, having established a good life for themselves and their children.

Decades before the Salem Witch Trials started in 1692, Puritan officials in the Massachusetts Bay Colony inflicted brutal punishments upon members of the Society of Friends, also known as Quakers. As the 1650s progressed, exceedingly harsh anti-Quaker laws went into effect from 1656–1658.[17] In some cases, the punishment was death by hanging on Boston Common. Governor John Endicott and his fellow Puritan authorities feared that if Quakers were given religious freedom to preach and live in the Massachusetts Bay Colony, then they would compromise the status quo, jeopardizing the Colony's future.

In 1656, Mary Dyer boarded a ship for the long journey home to Newport, Rhode Island, to reunite with her husband William and their six children. She had a long soujourn in England. Only Mary's second eldest son William Jr. shared her Quaker faith.[18] In subsequent generations, there were more Dyer family members who were Quakers. Mary would have been a virtual stranger upon her return to her youngest child Charles, as she had been away for most of his young life. She was around thirty-nine years old when he was born around 1650. He was possibly named after King Charles I, who was executed in January 1649 during the English Civil War. With Charles Dyer as my ancestor, I wondered what must it have been like for him to have his mother back in his life for such a short time before her death when he was ten years old. It was through Charles's family line that I have many Quaker ancestors as part of my family tree.

Mary's return to New England in 1657 could not have come at a worse time. The Massachusetts Bay Colony was enacting horrific punishments and discriminatory laws. Severe measures were being taken to drive Quakers out of the colony or to dissuade them from crossing the colony's borders in the first place. "In 1657, the court of Massachusetts imposed a fine of £100 on bringing a Quaker into that jurisdiction; and a Quaker returning after being sent away, to have one of his ears cut off; for a second offence, to lose the other ear. Every Quaker woman so returning, to be severely whipped, and for a third offence, to have her tongue bored through with a hot iron…But the laws already made, proving ineffectual, it was resolved to substitute, in some cases, even the punishment of death…In the colonies of Connecticut and New Haven, the enactments were less severe, and no one suffered death there for heresy."[19] All of these laws made Boston a dangerous port city for Mary to disembark after her long trip from London.

Mary returned home a changed woman, full of passion and conviction in the Quaker faith. She was supportive of her fellow Quakers. This religion that held that men and women were equal in the eyes of God was a sharp contrast to the Puritans' view of a chosen few pre-selected for salvation. Upon their reunion, Mary and her husband William would have to come to terms with their contrasting religious beliefs. William remained a Puritan while Mary internalized the Quaker belief in an "inner or inward light." For each individual, this inner light meant God's truths were revealed to them directly. Unlike their Puritan counterparts, Quakers did not rely on the sermons of a minister in a meeting house on Sabbath days to reveal the word of God. Puritan ministers and the officials who governed the Massachusetts Bay Colony felt such religious beliefs posed a serious threat. Quakers were persecuted in violent ways for their beliefs. "Quakers were singled out for very harsh punishment, partly because their religion [forbade] them from swearing oaths to the government or serving in the military. Just being a Quaker was punishable by whipping, mutilation, or death. Between 1658 and 1661, four Quakers were hanged."[20]

When the ship on which Mary had booked passage arrived in Boston Harbor, she had no way of knowing that both the Plymouth Colony and the Massachusetts Bay Colony had enacted anti-Quaker laws, including fines against sea captains who numbered Quakers among their passengers. "As the Quaker presence grew, the governors of Massachusetts Bay and Plymouth both took legal steps to prevent Quakers from entering their colonies. Under the Massachusetts Bay charter, the governor had no authority to imprison Quakers. In late 1656 and 1657, the General Court rectified this situation when it passed a series of laws that outlawed 'the cursed sect of heretics commonly called Quakers.' Captains of ships that brought Quakers to Massachusetts Bay were subject to heavy fines; so was anyone who owned books by Quakers or dared to defend the Quakers' 'devilish opinions.' "[21]

As a result of the new laws, Mary was denied a joyous reunion with her family. When the ship docked in Boston, she was thrown into prison along with her friend and fellow Quaker passenger, Anne Burden. For over two months, Mary sat in limbo in a prison cell. Far away in Newport, William eventually received word of his wife's fate. Puritan officials respected William Dyer. Only Mary had became a Quaker, while William maintained his Puritan faith. Massachusetts Bay Colony authorities did not have a problem with William because he did not become a Quaker. William rushed from Newport to Boston to meet with Governor John Endicott. In order to secure Mary's release, William was made to promise that he would ensure that Mary never ventured back to the Massachusetts Bay Colony. William was successful in freeing his wife, and she was finally reunited with her loved ones; however, being with her husband and children on their farm did not keep Mary safely at home and out of jail. She would find herself in a Boston prison cell two more times before her death in 1660.

It was not long before Mary made her way back to Boston during the summer of 1659 to visit and offer support to fellow Quakers William Robinson and Marmaduke Stevenson who were in jail. Having disobeyed the command to stay out of the colony, Mary was put in prison. Far away in Newport, William did what he could to again secure his wife's release. This time he penned a letter regarding the treatment and persecution of his wife, which he sent with great haste to the Court of Assistants in Boston. His letter highlighted the foul and unjust treatment of his wife. "Had you no commiseration of a tender soul that being wett to the skin, you cause her to [be] thrust into a room whereon was nothing to sitt or lye down upon but dust…had your dogg been wett you would have offered it the liberty of a chimney corner to dry itself, or had your hoggs been pend in a sty…but alas, Christians now with you are used worse [than] hoggs or doggs…oh merciless cruelties."[22]

William did not shy away from pointing out that his wife had been in Boston solely to visit her imprisoned friends. She had not come to disturb or disrupt the daily goverance of the colony.

> [She] only came to visit her friends in prison and when dispatching that her intent of returning to her family as she declared in her (statement) the next day to the Governor, therefore it is you that disturbed her, else why was she not let alone…She was about a business justifiable before God and all good men? …What hath not people in America the same liberty as beasts and birds to pass the land or air without examination?[23]

William's letter did not secure Mary's release from jail. She languished in her cell from the end of August 1659 until a meeting of the Massachusetts General Court in October 1659. Mary, William Robinson, and Marmaduke Stevenson all appeared before the Council of State where Governor Endicott handed down a verdict of death by hanging, as no other means of keeping these Quakers out of the colony had been effective.[24] After being taken back to her jail cell, Mary penned the only two letters of hers that survive to this day. In the first letter to the General Court, Mary wrote,

Search with the light of Christ in you, and it will show you of whom, as it hath done me, and many more, who have been disobedient and deceived, as now you are, which Light, as you come into, and obey what is made manifest to you therein, you will not repent, that you were kept from shedding Blood tho be a Woman: It's not my own Life I seek (for I chose rather to suffer with the People of God, than to enjoy the Pleasures of Egypt) but the Life of the Seed, which I know the Lord hath blessed, and therefore seeks the Enemy thus vehmently the Life thereof to destroy, as in all ages he ever did...[25]

She ended her letter written in her cell with these words, "In Love and in the Spirit of Meekness, I again beseech you, for I have no Enmity to the Persons of any; but you shall know, that God will not be mocked, but what you sow, that shall you reap from him, that will render to everyone according to the Deeds done in the Body, whether Good or Evil, Even so be it, saith."[26] Mary prayed and prepared to die. On October 27, 1659, she, William Robinson, and Marmaduke Stevenson were taken from their jail cells to be hanged. William and Marmaduke were executed first, then "Mary Dyer, her arms and legs bound and the halter around her neck, received a prearranged last-minute reprieve as a result of intercession by Gov. John Winthrop, Jr. of Connecticut and Gov. Thomas Temple of Nova Scotia and a plea from her son William."[27]

William Jr.'s petition had helped influence Governor Endicott to spare his mother. The experience of preparing herself for death only to be spared while her friends were killed, left Mary full of conviction when she penned the only other letter of hers to survive. This letter was written to the Massachusetts General Court.

I rather chuse to die than to live, as from you, as Guilty of their innocent Blood. Therefore, seeing my Request is hindered, I leave you to the Righteous Judge and Searcher of all Hearts, who, with the pure measure of Light he hath given to every Man to profit withal, will in his due time let you see whose Servants you are, and of whom you have taken Counsel...When I heard your last Order read it was a disturbance unto me, that was so freely Offering up my life to him that give it me, and sent me hither to do, which Obedience being his own Work, he gloriously accompanied with his Presence, and Peace, and Love

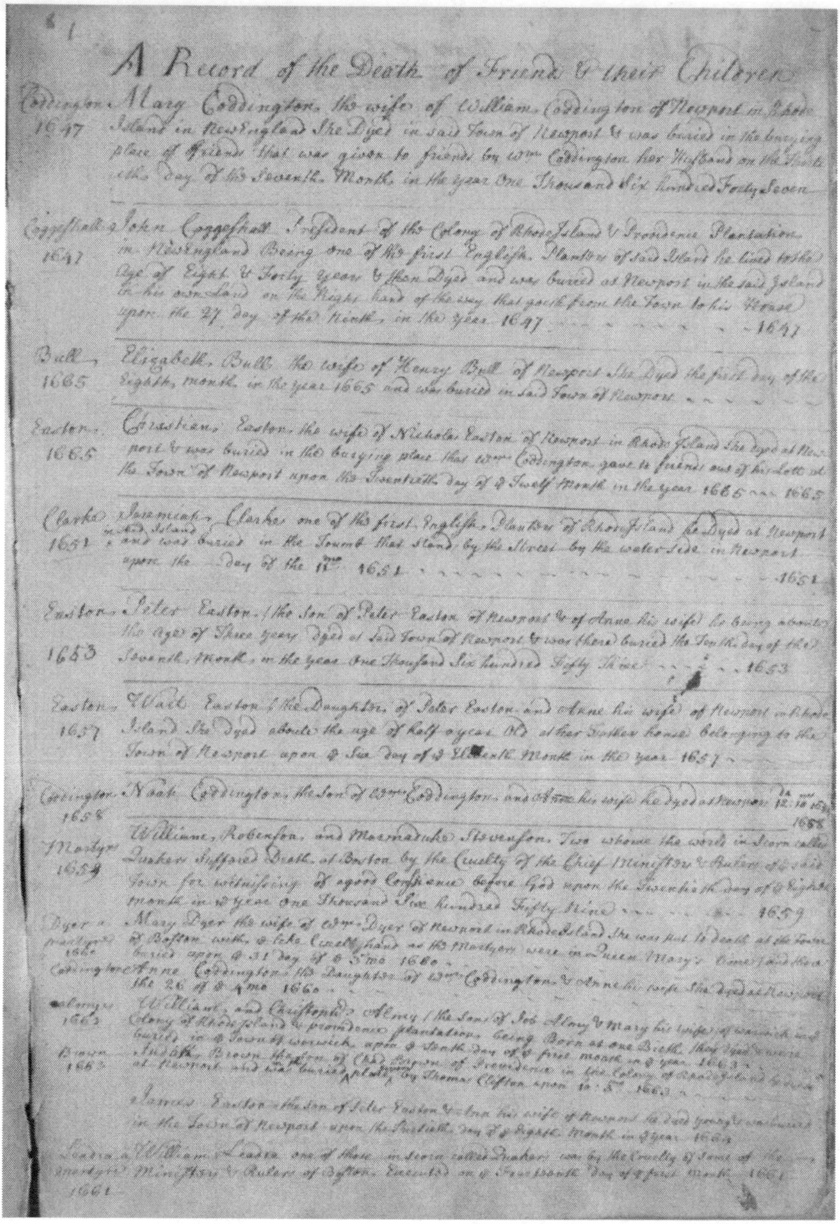

61

A Record of the Death of Friends & their Children

Coddington 1647 — Mary Coddington the wife of William Coddington of Newport in Rhode Island in New England She Dyed in said Town of Newport & was buried in the burying place of friends that was given to friends by Wm Coddington her Husband on the Tenth day of the Seventh Month in the year One Thousand Six hundred Forty Seven

Coggeshall 1647 — John Coggeshall President of the Colony of Rhode Island & Providence Plantation in New England Being one of the first English Planters of said Island he lived to the Age of Eight & Forty years & then Dyed and was buried at Newport in the said Island in his own Land on the Right hand of the way that goeth from the Town to his House upon the 27 day of the Ninth in the year 1647 — 1647

Bull 1665 — Elizabeth Bull the wife of Henry Bull of Newport She Dyed the first day of the Eighth month in the year 1665 and was buried in said Town of Newport

Easton 1665 — Christian Easton the wife of Nicholas Easton of Newport in Rhode Island She dyed at Newport & was buried in the burying place that Wm Coddington gave to friends out of his Lott at the Town of Newport upon the Tuentieth day of ye Twelf Month in the year 1665 — 1665

Clarke 1651 — Jeremiah Clarke one of the first English Planters of Rhode Island he Dyed at Newport in said Island and was buried in the Toumb that stands by the Street by the water side in Newport upon the — day of the 11mo 1651 — 1651

Easton 1653 — Peter Easton (the Son of Peter Easton of Newport & of Anne his wife) he being about the Age of Three years dyed at said Town of Newport & was there buried the Tenth day of the Seventh Month in the year One Thousand Six hundred Fifty Three — 1653

Easton 1657 — Elizabeth Easton (the Daughter of Peter Easton and Anne his wife) of Newport in Rhode Island She dyed about the age of half a year old at her Father house belonging to the Town of Newport upon ye Six day of ye Eleventh Month in the year 1657

Coddington 1658 — Noah Coddington the Son of Wm Coddington and Anne his wife he dyed at Newport 12: 10mo 1658 — 1658

Martyrs 1659 — William Robenson and Marmaduke Stevenson Two whome the world in Scorn called Quakers Suffered Death at Boston by the Cruelty of the Chief Ministers & Rulers of said Town for witnessing of a good Conscience before God upon the Twentieth day of ye Eighth month in ye year One Thousand Six hundred Fifty Nine — 1659

Dyer a Martyr 1660 — Mary Dyer the wife of Wm Dyer of Newport in Rhode Island She was put to death at the Town of Boston with ye like Cruelty hand as the Martyrs were in Queen Mary's time [illegible] buried upon ye 31 day of ye 3mo 1660.

Coddington — Anne Coddington the Daughter of Wm Coddington & Anne his wife She dyed at Newport the 26 of ye 4mo 1660.

Almy 1663 — William and Christopher Almy (the Sons of Job Almy & Mary his wife) of Warwick in ye Colony of Rhode Island & Providence plantation being Born at one Birth they dyed & were buried in ye Town of Warwick upon ye Sixth day of ye first month in ye year 1663.

Brown 1663 — Judith Brown the [illegible] of Providence in the Colony of Rhode Island [illegible] at Newport and was buried [illegible] place by Thomas Clifton upon 10: 5mo 1663.

James Easton the Son of Peter Easton & Anne his wife of Newport he dyed young & was buried in the Town of Newport upon the [illegible] day of ye Eight Month in ye year 166[illegible]

Leddra a Martyr 1661 — William Leddra one of those in scorn called Quakers was by the Cruelty of Some of the Ministers & Rulers of Boston Executed on ye Fourteenth day of ye first Month 1661

18th century Society of Friends (Quaker) record of the deaths in their community. This record includes an entry of Mary Dyer's execution. This entry was written about seventy years after her death. Image courtesy of the Newport Historical Society, Newport, Rhode Island.

in me, in which I rested from my labour, till by your Order, and the People, I was so far disturbed, that I could not retain anymore of the words thereof, than I should return to Prison, and there remain Forty and Eight hours...[28]

In April 1660, Mary made the fateful decision to return to Boston in direct violation of the terms upon which her reprieve had been granted. This time her family could do nothing to spare her from the gallows. Her husband William wrote one last time to Governor Endicott on May 27, 1660, closing with a heartful plea to spare the life of his wife of almost thirty years and mother of his children. "But I pray give her me once agen and I shall bee so much obleiged for ever, that I shall endeavor continually to utter my thanks and render you Love and Honor most renowed: pitty me, I begg itt with teares, and rest you."[29] William's words could not save his wife. She was again taken from her jail cell to the gallows. On June 1, 1660, Mary died a martyr's death at the end of a hangman's noose on Boston Common. Mary was forty-nine years old. "She hangs there," remarked an unsympathetic bystander, "as a flag for others to take example by." This quote was shared on the website Minerdescent.com.

The history of the Sandwich, Massachusetts, Quaker meetings noted the influence of Quakers in England on King Charles II. "Quakers in England, some of whom were very prominent and well-connected, got his ear and told him the horrible things that were happening, especially in Massachusetts Bay, and got him to issue an edict that there should be no more killings, and that the people charged with major Quaker crimes should be sent to England whereby a process of appeals and so on, things could be eased for them."[30] Mary Dyer's intention was to be an example, " 'a witness' in the Quaker sense, for freedom of conscience."[31] Her death had not been in vain, for it helped influenced King Charles II after he was restored to the English throne in 1660.

On a brisk Sunday morning in early February 2012, I found myself on Boston Common, bundled up in a long warm wool coat and winter boots. With a hot coffee, I strolled, lost in thought about the past. The crisp air was punctured with the barks of dogs happily frolicking on the frozen ground, their owners tossing balls for them to fetch.

Basking in wintery sunshine, I realized 351 years had passed since Mary's execution near the Frog Pond on the Common. It was a short walk across the Common to reach a vantage point where I could view Mary's statue on the west lawn of the State House. I thought to myself how Mary would smile at the irony that, "In 1959 by the authority of the Massachusetts General Court, which had condemned her nearly 300 years before, a statue was erected in her memory on the grounds of the State House in Boston."[32] Gazing at her bronze image, I thought about her life. She was a daughter, educated woman, wife, mother, Quaker, preacher, and martyr. I felt tremendous love and respect for her and for her decision to stand up for what she believed was just.

Two days later on Valentine's Day, 2012, I drove to Newport. My excitement escalated the closer I got to my destination. At the Newport Historical Society, Bert Lippincott, the reference librarian and genealogist, added to the information I found through my own research on the Dyer family, their lives in seventeenth-century Newport, and Mary's Quaker faith. Lippincott discussed both the settlement of Newport and the beliefs of Quakers, which troubled Puritan authorities in the Massachusetts Bay Colony. An important point he raised was the Quaker belief in an "Inward Light," which meant individuals felt a direct personal connection to God. This was a threatening concept to the Puritan authorities of the Massachusetts Bay Colony, where there was no separation between church and state, and authorities wanted it to stay that way.

My research visit helped make this particular Valentine's Day memorable in a special way. I viewed Mary's signature on a land deed she and William had signed; they each had spelled "Dyer" a different way. This was the first time that I viewed an original document signed by a female ancestor. In the seventeenth century, many women did not learn how to read, write, or even how to sign their own names. The other historic record I viewed that trip was a Quaker records book containing an entry about Mary's execution in 1660. The word "martyr" was written beside her name in black ink. I felt goose bumps run down my skin as I stared at the word "martyr," which looked as though the script was newly penned, not over three hundred years old. Being referred to as a martyr by those who shared Mary's faith meant her death had not been in vain. The strength of her convictions stood out both to those who loved her and to those who were against her.

Inspired by all I had learned about Mary and William Dyer, I wanted to know more about my Quaker ancestors bearing the last names of Underhill, Townsend, and Wright. These ancestors had settled in Oyster Bay, New York, and over the centuries marriages and kinship bound these families tightly together.

Early one overcast August morning in August 2012, I traveled for the first time on a research trip, not by land or by air but by sea. Boarding the Cross Sound Ferry in New London, I thought about Joshua Hempstead and other ancestors who had often made similar journeys across Long Island Sound to Long Island. I was excited to see the North Fork of Long Island for the first time, as Joshua's wife Abigail Bailey was born and raised in Southold, Long Island. Having seen the home where she and Joshua raised their family in New London, I was excited at the prospect of driving around the area she had once called home. But my exploration of Southold would have to wait for another day.

This trip allowed me to observe aspects of my ancestors' lives starting with crossing Long Island Sound by boat and then driving through areas intimately connected with my ancestors and their daily lives. In the sixteen hundreds, both Oyster Bay and Shelter Island offered places of refuge for my Quaker ancestors. These locations were far removed from the violent persecutions Quakers suffered elsewhere. When my ancestors sought sanctuary, they were lucky to find it and to share it with other like-minded individuals on Long Island.

Finding myself on Shelter Island had not been on my travel itinerary. I naively thought I was going to travel by ferry from New London, Connecticut, to Orient Point, New York, and then I would drive on dry land the rest of the way to Oyster Bay. I thought my car's navigation system was broken when it kept directing me to a parking lot on a harbor. I suddenly realized that I was going to board a ferry with only a few minutes remaing to board. Not sure what to expect, I crossed my fingers tightly and inched my car forward onto the small North Ferry. The ferry transported me from Greenport, New York, to Shelter Island, which was the location where I would board another ferry to go to the South Fork of Long Island.

As soon as my car was parked on the North Ferry, I was asked to produce payment for the ride. I had neither cash nor checks, having already paid for my Cross Sound Ferry ticket from New London with a credit card. I was unprepared for this request and unclear if I would be able to finish this research trip! Luckily, I unearthed just enough coins to pay the fare, and I was free to leave the ferry when it docked at Shelter Island.

The heavens opened as I drove onto the island. My first impressions were a sea of green foliage. As light rain fell, the mainland felt a million miles away. A quiet peacefulness pervaded in the midst of this lush forest of trees and cottages dotting the road. There were no long lines of cars or the busy hustle and bustle of New London or Greenport boarding ferries.

Though I admired its beauty, what I took away from Shelter Island was not a memory of a view or a seaside home; it was a fact I read on a historic plaque mentioning Nathaniel Sylvester, who settled there with his wife Gissell in 1652. They were the only white settlers on the island, and they had both African slaves and Native Americans working on their property. The Sylvesters were not my ancestors, but they were connected to George Fox whom they met in England. After meeting Fox, the Sylvesters were kind to Quakers in the 1650s. Fox inspired my ancestor Mary Dyer to become a Quaker during her time in England in the 1650s.

Shelter island had direct connections to my search for my Quaker connections to Long Island. Mary Dyer spent some of the last months of her life on the island. She benefitted from the hospitality of Gissell and Nathaniel Sylvester, as she chose to stay with them rather than with her family in Newport, Rhode Island. Mary's close brush with death in October 1659 had left her contemplating what she would do with her life and what her purpose in this world might be.

On Shelter Island, Mary preached to a gathering of Native Americans and African slaves brought from Barbados by Nathaniel Sylvester to work on his land. Mary was the first female preacher I found on my family tree among a group of five other male ancestors who were ministers or deacons of New England churches. "Quaker women were exceptional in the equality afforded them in both the theory and practice of religion, and when Dyer returned to America in 1657, she set about exercising her church's unusual use of women as missionaries for the humane new faith."[33]

A fellow Quaker named John Taylor attended one of Mary's meetings. His impression of Mary and the meeting was of "a comely woman and a grave matron who even shined in the image of God, we had several brave meetings there [in Shelter Island] together, and the Lord's power and preference were with us generously."[34] Learning that Mary's time on Shelter Island offered her opportunity to enjoy peace and solace and to share her faith with others comforted me. She left the island in April 1660, and she would never see it again.

During her time on Shelter Island, Mary felt called to go back to Boston to stand up for her Quaker beliefs. She knew her return to Boston meant certain death. Mary's time on the island did not separate her from the persecution of Quakers in Boston. She felt connected to the sufferings of fellow Quakers, and in turn she internalized their persecutions and torments.

This particular trip forged more of my ancestral connections to George Fox, the founder of the Quaker religion. Many of my early Quaker ancestors found themselves influenced by Fox during the early years of Quakerism. In 1672, George Fox visited Oyster Bay and met with my Wright, Underhill, and Feake ancestors. Fox's interaction with many of my ancestors, who became Quakers early on, made him a central figure in their lives, and in turn, it became part of the larger story of my family roots in America. My journey to Shelter Island and Oyster Bay revealed the surprising discovery that my maternal grandparents had ancestors who were inspired by Fox to become Quakers.

The purpose of my research trip had been to uncover my own Quaker roots and connections to Oyster Bay. Somehow I had forgotten Mary's connections to Shelter Island when I visited. My search for my early Quaker heritage had put me unknowingly on a direct path to Shelter Island; two branches of research came together in one location.

As I researched my Quaker ancestors, the question arose, what would happen if a married couple in the Massachusetts Bay Colony both converted to the Quaker faith in the 1650s and were then persecuted? What would happen to children if both parents were imprisoned, fined, or tortured for being Quakers?

Answers to these questions came from researching my Harper ancestors, who lived in Sandwich, Massachusetts, in the 1650s. Sandwich was part of Plymouth Bay Colony, not Massachusetts Bay Colony; each colony had its own rules to reprimand Quakers. My ancestors Robert and Deborah (Perry) Harper had the misfortune of being persecuted in both Plymouth Bay Colony and Massachusetts Bay Colony. Fines, whippings, and imprisonment were heaped upon them as they valiantly supported their fellow Quakers while raising a family and tending home and hearth.

The following points are some of the incidences of fines, whippings, and incarcerations of Robert Harper:

I June 1658 – Robert was fined £10 at Plymouth for failure to take the "oath of fidelitie." (Ten pounds could purchase a calf or colt, so it was a considerable penalty in that economy.)

2 Oct 1658 – Robert was fined £5 for refusing to take the "oath of fidelitie," along with twelve others of Sandwich.

7 Jun 1659 – Robert and other Quakers appeared before the Plymouth court for failure to take the "oath of fidelitie," and [was] fined £5.

6 Oct 1659 – Robert appeared before the court for failure to take the "oath of fidelitie," and [was] fined £5 at Plymouth. A month later, Mary Dyer visited Sandwich.

8 or 13 June 1660- Robert was fined £5 for refusing to take the "oath of fidelitie."

2 Oct 1660 – Robert was convicted for refusing to take the "oath of fidelitie," at the General Court in Plymouth; [he was] fined £6 at Plymouth.

2 Oct 1660 – Robert and Deborah Harper were fined £4, "for being att Quakers meetings."

13 Oct 1660 – Robert and Deborah Harper and others visit Quaker friends in Salem's jail, [they were] arrested and committed to Boston's House of Correction. They petitioned for release on 24 Dec 1660, but no record is noted of their disposition at that time.

24 Mar 1661 – Robert, who had been only recently released from Boston prison, "stood under the scaffold and caught in his arms the body of his friend William Leddra, the martyr preacher," when Leddra's hanging rope was cut. For this, he and his wife were banished from Massachusetts Bay Colony (different jurisdiction from Plymouth Colony). In late June/early July 1661, an order from King Charles II arrived in Massachusetts that stopped executions for religion's sake. It also had the effect of reducing (though not stopping) persecution of the Quakers.

1663 – Robert was sentenced to be "publickly whipt for his intollerable insolent disturbance, both for the congregation of Barnstable and Sandwich."

1670 – Again the same sentence was passed upon Robert Harper "for reviling Mr. Walley," minister of Barnstable.[35]

In the span of a few short years, Robert and Deborah survived imprisonment, fines, Robert's whipping, and banishment from Massachusetts Bay Colony. During the latter part of 1660 and the beginning of 1661, Robert's persecutions and suffering escalated as both he and his wife were taken away from their children and imprisoned. Robert witnessed the execution of his friend, William Leddra, catching William's body in his arms when he was cut down from the scaffold.

Despite all the horrific punishments inflicted upon him, Robert remained one of the more fortunate Quakers, as he did not have an ear cut off. The Massachusetts Bay Colony authorities inflicted this torture on some Quakers. In the midst of the turmoil and persecution, Robert and Deborah started a family. Their children suffered dearly, and they came close to losing both parents during this frightening period of persecution. "Robert and Deborah Harper had two young children at the time of their Quaker activism and persecution. Mary Harper was born 25 Dec 1655, and Experience was born Nov 1657. Possibly the little girls were kept by their Perry grandparents. They grew up to marry and bear a tribe of Quakers. Deborah Perry Harper, their mother, died shortly after giving birth to a baby in December 1665."[36] The prospect that the little Harper girls could have lost both parents must have sobered those caring for them when their parents were put in prison. My ancestor Experience Harper was just three years old when her parents were imprisoned, and she was only eight years old when her mother Deborah died in childbirth.

The spirit of activism and passion embodied by both the Harpers and Mary Dyer was imprinted in the minds and in the genetics of their children and grandchildren. After all of the hardships faced by their parents, life was not necessarily easier for the children of these first Quaker converts. Mary Dyer's children living in Rhode Island benefitted from being able to worship as they pleased.

For Experience Harper, a settled family life was not to be until she and her husband moved to Rhode Island from their home in Falmouth, Massachusetts. In 1676, Experience married Joseph Hull, who was also a staunch defender of Quakers and their right to worship freely. Their first years of married life echoed that of her parents because the persecution of Quakers had not ceased. Joseph was defiant like his father, Captain Tristram Hull, who did not share the Quaker faith, but supported Quakers whenever he could. Captain Hull was a well-respected active member of the Barnstable, Massachusetts, community, where he frequently participated as a juror and served on the town's board of selectmen.[37] His involvement in town affairs and politics did not spare him from fines imposed when he aided or supported Quakers. Given Tristram's support of Quakers, during his life it was not surprising to discover his son Joseph became a Quaker and married a Quaker.

My Quaker family tree branched out considerably when my ancestor Joseph married into the Harper family. "At about the time Joseph Hull and Experience Harper were married, the magistrates of Massachusetts undertook without due process of law to release bondservants and cancel articles of apprenticeship, where the masters were Quakers. In the execution of some such ex-party order, the sheriff was soundly thrashed by Joseph Hull, who, for so doing was fined seven pounds. This fine, for some unstated reason, was abated at a subsequent session of the court."[38]

Experience's father Robert Harper passed away in 1704, so he knew of the ill-treatment his son-in-law Joseph Hull suffered in Falmouth. Robert's long life[39] meant that he was alive when his grandson Tristram Hull married Elizabeth Dyer, a granddaughter of Mary Dyer, on February 9, 1699, at the Friends' Meeting House in Newport, Rhode Island. The year Tristram and Elizabeth were married marked almost forty years since his grandfather Robert had witnessed the execution of William Leddra. The marriage of my ancestors Tristram and Elizabeth united two early Quaker families in New England. Their descendants on my branch of the family tree lived in Rhode Island until the 1770s, when they moved to Connecticut.

Author's photos taken in August 2012 of Council Rock where George Fox (founder of the Quaker religion) preached in May 1672 during his visit to Oyster Bay, New York. Allison Putala, director of the Townsend Society of America is pictured standing beside Council Rock. Ms. Putala took the author on a tour of Underhill and Townsend sites in Oyster Bay. The interpretive marker pictured was erected in 1939. The author's Quaker ancestors who gathered here to listen to Fox likely included Captain John Underhill who passed away just a few months later in July 1672, John's second wife Elizabeth (Feake) Underhill, and their daughter (also an ancestor of the author) Deborah (later Deborah (Underhill) Townsend after her marriage to Henry Townsend II). The author wondered if her ancestor Henry Townsend, who signed The Flushing Remonstrance, also came to hear Fox speak. Henry Townsend had a mill near this location and he was buried in close proximity to Council Rock in the Mill Hill Cemetery.

CHAPTER

five

The Flushing Remonstrance

In the 1650s, the Massachusetts Bay Colony was not the only place where Quakers were unwelcome and persecuted for their religious beliefs. While researching my Townsend and Underhill ancestors in Oyster Bay, New York, I learned about an important document from 1657—*The Flushing Remonstrance*. Thirty men signed this document, including my ancestors Henry and John Townsend, to protest the persecution of Quakers in the seventeenth-century colony of New Netherland.

Henry Townsend, along with his brothers John and Richard, emigrated to America sometime before 1645 during a period of deep unrest and conflict in England, as the English Civil War was escalating there. To date, there has been no consensus on the location of their home in England. A nineteenth-century history of the Townsend brothers and their family lines stated they came from Norwich, County of Norfolk, England.[1] In his history of Long Island, also published in the nineteenth century, Benjamin F. Thompson wrote of the brothers' origins that "John and Henry Townsend, with their brother, Richard, emigrated, it is believed, from Lynn Regis, in Norfolkshire, England, to Saugus, (now Lynn), Massachusetts, a little previous to 1640, and soon after arrived in the New Netherlands."[2] Allison Putala, director of the Townsend Society of America, shared what came from research into the English origins of the family. "There have been conjectures about where they came from, but no proof of any kind. The editor of our newsletter [Townsend Society Genealogical Journal], Liane Fenimore, has been systematically searching baptisms in England, and of course, started with Norwich. Nothing. Nothing in the surrounding areas, either. So as of right now [2013], we don't know where they came from, nor who their father was."[3]

Of the three brothers, Richard had the least written about him in *A Memorial of John, Henry, and Richard Townsend, and Their Descendants*, published in 1865. The first records in it of Richard's whereabouts in New England placed him in Jamaica, Long Island, in 1656. Then his name appeared in Oyster Bay, Long Island, records in 1668.[4] Likely around 1652,[5] Richard married his first wife, Deliverance Coles,[6] the eldest daughter of Robert Coles. His brother (my ancestor) Henry married her younger sister Ann Coles a year later in 1653[7]. It is possible that their brother (also my ancestor) John Townsend and his wife Elizabeth Montgomery were parents-in-law to Sarah Coles, who was the youngest child of Robert Coles and his second wife Mary (Hawkshurst) Coles. Sarah Coles was identified in a 1901 publication as the wife of Thomas Townsend.[8] Henry and Richard married the Coles sisters in the early 1650s, so they likely met Robert Coles and his family after they moved to Warwick, Rhode Island, around 1653 from Providence. John and Henry Townsend moved to Warwick in the late 1640s or early 1650s from Vlissengen, New Netherland. *A Memorial of John, Henry, and Richard* noted that all three brothers were "members of the Provincial Assembly, besides holding municipal offices."[9] The three brothers attended sessions of the Provincial Assembly in Rhode Island.

Long before moving to Rhode Island, John and Henry Townsend initially resided in Vlissengen (now Flushing, Queens). Vlissengen was part of the Dutch colony of New Netherland, which was composed of "a series of trading posts, towns, and forts up and down the Hudson River that laid the groundwork for towns that still exist today. Fort Orange, the northernmost of the Dutch outposts, is known today as Albany; New York City's original name was New Amsterdam, and the New Netherland's third major settlement, Wiltwyck, is known today as Kingston."[10] Many residents of Vlissengen were English settlers. Vlissengen proved a difficult place for John and Henry to live for a long period, as they did not share the same views as the Dutch authorities.

John had difficulty in settling into his new home. Governor Stuyvesant named him as one of the individuals "who resist the Dutch mode of choosing Sheriff, pretending against the adopted course in the Fatherland, and who refuse to contribute their share to the maintenance of Christian, pious, reformed ministers."[11] John's unwillingness to support and cooperate with Dutch rules caused him, along with other residents of Vlissengen,[12] to be "summoned to appear, 23rd of January, 1648, before the Director-General, Governor, and Council, at Fort Amsterdam. If they decline[d], they [would have been] apprehended and prosecuted by the Attorney-General."[13] Fort Amsterdam was built, "in the south point of Manhattan island, at the junction of the East and North rivers."[14] The reprimand from the authorities drove John and Henry to leave Vlissengen, seeking refuge in Rhode Island.

The Townsend brothers did not settle in Rhode Island permanently. In 1656, Henry, John, and Richard returned to the colony of New Netherland. They moved to the new settlement of Rusdorp, which was renamed Jamaica when the English took control in 1664. "Jamaica, one of the oldest settlements within the boundaries of New York City, developed into the leading commercial and entertainment center of Queens County. The southern part of the area was inhabited by a Native American tribe called Jameco (or Jemaco) when the first Europeans arrived there in 1655. In 1656, [my ancestor] Robert Jackson applied to Governor Stuyvesant for a patent and 'purchased' ten acres of land from the native tribe and called the settlement Rusdorp."[15]

Only a year after returning to New Netherland, Henry found himself in trouble with Dutch authorities. He was penalized on the 15 September 1657 for "'having called together conventicles;'" he was ordered to pay a fine of £8 Flanders or else to depart the province within six weeks, upon the penalty of corporeal punishment."[16] Thompson's *History of Long Island* noted that by late December 1657 Henry had not paid the fine of £8 Flanders. It remains a mystery to me how he managed to stay in the province from September 1657 to December 1657 when he signed *The Flushing Remonstrance*.

A conventicle is "a secret or unauthorized meeting, especially for religious worship, as those held by Protestant dissenters in England in the 16th and 17th centuries" or "a place of meeting or assembly, especially a Nonconformist meeting house."[17] An unpublished family record (shared with me by a cousin) mentioned that Henry was "found guilty of having Quaker meetings in his home."[18] Thompson's *History of Long Island* said, "on the 29th of December 1657, the magistrates of Rusdorp informed the governor that the [Q]uakers and their adherents were lodged, and entertained, and unrelentingly corresponded in said village, at the house of Henry Townsend; who, they say formerly convocated a conventicle of the [Q]uakers, and assisted in it, for which he had been condemned on the 15th of September, 1657, in an amende of £8 Flanders, that had not as yet been paid."[19]

Henry's religious sympathies got him into trouble for having "convocated a conventicle of Quakers." The 1865 history of the Townsend brothers published in New York by W. A. Townsend stated that the Townsends were "Friends"[20] by the time they signed *The Flushing Remonstrance*. Thompson's *History of Long Island*, published over twenty years earlier, documented the persecution of Henry in the wake of his signing *The Flushing Remonstrance*. The book acknowledged that Henry supported Quakers but did not conclusively state that he was a Quaker. Whether or not Henry and his brother John were Quakers when they signed *The Flushing Remonstrance* was not something that could be conclusively determined. It is probable that Henry and possibly John were already Quakers by 1657. It is also probable that their strong support for the Quaker religion and their sympathies for Quakers, who were being persecuted, later inspired them to become Quakers. Henry's exposure to Quakers and to their religious views when they held meetings in his home make it likely that he became a Quaker sometime after 1657 when he moved his family to Oyster Bay, Long Island.

Along with his brother John, Henry was one of the thirty signers of *The Flushing Remonstrance*; other signers included the sheriff, town clerk, and two magistrates of Flushing.[21] Henry's decision to sign was influenced by the Quakers he had met and whom he had allowed to gather in his home. He felt they should be able to worship freely without persecution, and he did not support the regulations enforced by the Dutch authorities governing the colony of New Netherland.

There were residents of Flushing brave enough to allow Quakers to hold their meetings in their homes. Dutch authorities did not welcome Quakers. Strict regulations were enforced to dissuade Quakers from coming to the area, and to motivate Quakers already residing in New Netherland to move elsewhere. "Largely settled by English families, Vlissengen proved to be fertile ground for Quakers who were persecuted at home in England. Quaker religious teachings spread throughout Vlissengen (known today as Flushing, Queens) and Long Island, threatening the dominance of the Dutch Reformed Church in New Netherland. Consequently, Peter Stuyvesant, the governor of New Netherland, forbade colonists from allowing Quaker meetings to be held in any home."[22] As Henry discovered, punishments for hosting Quakers included large fines and imprisonment.

On December 27, 1657, Henry and John gathered together with men from the town of Vlissengen to sign *The Flushing Remonstrance*, which they sent to the Dutch Governor of New Netherland, Peter Stuyvesant. Remonstrance means "an earnest presentation of reasons for opposition or grievance; *especially*: a document formally stating such points."[23] A remonstrance was a "traditional form of Dutch protest."[24] This remonstrance was drafted to protest "the policy of Peter Stuyvesant, the provincial director general, that restricted the worship of Quakers because they were not members of the Dutch Reformed Church."[25] *The Flushing Remonstrance* expressed principles that were later incorporated into the first amendment of the United States Constitution. The signers of the remonstrance were aware of the risks and repercussions involved with their signatures or marks appearing on this document. They addressed Governor Stuyvesant:

> You have been pleased to send unto us a certain prohibition or command that we should not receive or entertain any of those people called Quakers because they are supposed to be, by some, seducers of the people. For our part we cannot condemn them in this case, neither can we stretch out our hands against them, for out of Christ God is a consuming fire, and it is a fearful thing to fall into the hands of the living God.
>
> Wee desire therefore in this case not to judge least we be judged, neither to condemn least we be condemned, but rather let every man stand or fall to his own Master. Wee are bounde by the law to do good unto all men, especially to those of the household of faith. And though for the present we seem to be unsensible for the law and the Law giver, yet when death and the Law assault us, if wee have our advocate to seeke, who shall plead for us in this case of conscience betwixt God and our own souls; the powers of this world can neither attach us, neither excuse us, for if God justifye who can condemn and if God condemn there is none can justifye.

They clearly stated why New Netherland should permit Quakers and others the freedom to freely worship and not require them to attend the Dutch Reformed Church in the colony.

The law of love, peace, and liberty in the states extending to
Jews, Turks, and Egyptians, as they are considered sons of
Adam, which is the glory of the outward state of Holland, soe
love, peace and liberty, extending to all in Christ Jesus,
condemns hatred, war, and bondage. And because our Saviour
sayeth it is impossible but that offences will come, but woe unto
him by whom they cometh, our desire is not to offend one of
his little ones, in whatsoever form, name or title hee appears in,
whether Presbyterian, Independent, Baptist or Quaker, but shall
be glad to see anything of God in any of them, desiring to doe
unto all men as we desire all men should doe unto us, which is
the true law both of Church and State; for our Saviour sayeth
this is the law and the prophets.[26]

The thirty individuals who signed this document sent to the
governor a bold statement that "All men should doe unto us, which is the
true law both of Church and State; for our Saviour sayeth this is the law
and the prophets."[27] What stood out about this particular line was that,
"In Biblical language, the document cited divine authority as superseding
human authority."[28] The statement that "divine authority" surpassed
"human authority" was certain to disturb Governor Stuyvesant. "These
English nationals, subject to Dutch law, signed the document on Dec. 27,
1657. After they presented it to the colonial government, some of them
were arrested (and released a short time later)."[29]

The signatures of Henry Townsend and his brother John did
not escape the notice of the governor. "He [Henry], the clerk, and
magistrates were arrested, and John Townsend also, upon a charge of
having induced the magistrates to sign, and he was ordered to find bail
in £12, to appear when summoned. Henry was brought before the
Council, January 15th, 1658, and condemned to £100 Flanders, and to
remain arrested until it be paid. We are not told how this was settled;
but he was in Oyster Bay during this year, as his signature as witness to
an Indian deed proves."[30]

Thompson's *History of Long Island* also discussed Henry's precarious
position in January 1658 with the detail that Henry's punishment would
serve as an example to other would-be offenders.

On the 15th of Jan. 1658, Henry Townsend was again brought
before the council, and the farce ended by the attorney general,

declaring, that as the prisoner had before and now again, trespassed and treated with contempt the placards of the director general and the council in New Netherlands, in lodging quakers, which he unconditionally confessed, he should therefore, be condemned in an amende of £100 Flanders, as an example for other transgressors and contumelious offenders, of the good order and placards of the director general and council in New Netherlands, and so to remain arrested till the said amende be paid, besides the costs and mises of justice.[31]

The signers risked fines, imprisonment, and possible banishment because they believed there should be religious tolerance in the colony. In the years after signing *The Flushing Remonstrance*, Henry resettled his family in Oyster Bay, Long Island, where many members of his family, including his son Henry Jr. and his wife Deborah (Underhill) Townsend, were members of the Society of Friends.

NEVVES FROM

AMERICA;

OR,

A NEW AND EXPERI-

MENTALL DISCOVERIE OF

New England;

CONTAINING,

A TRVE RELATION OF THEIR

War-like proceedings thefe two yeares laft
paft, with a Figure of the Indian Fort,
or Palizado.

Alfo a difcovery of thefe
places, that as yet have
very few or no Inhabi-
tants which would yeeld   Viz.
fpeciall accommodation
to fuch as will Plant
there.

- Queenapoick,
- Agu-wom,
- Hudfon's River.
- Long Ifland.
- Nahanticut.
- Martins Vinyard.
- Pequet.
- Naranfett Bay,
- Elizabeth Iflands.
- Pufcataway.
- Casko, with about a hun-
  dred Iflands neere to
  Casko.

By Captaine IOHN UNDERHILL, a Commander
in the Warres there.

LONDON,
Printed by J.D. for Peter Cole, and are to be fold at the figne
of the Glove in Corne-hill neere the
Royall Exchange, 1638.

Copy of cover from original edition of Captain John Underhill's "Newes From America"
published in London, England in 1638. This original copy of Underhill's account of the
Pequot War is held in the collections of the Houghton Library, Harvard University,
Cambridge, Massachusetts and its call number is STC 24518.

The Pequot War

The Pequot War was a pivotal and bloody conflict in the early years of settlement in colonial New England. The conflict took place in 1637, just seventeen years after the *Mayflower* anchored off the coast of Cape Cod. The Pequots were:

"an Algonquian tribe of Connecticut. Before their conquest by the English in 1637 they were the most dreaded of the southern New England tribes. They were originally but one people with the Mohegan, and it is possible that the term Pequot was unknown until applied by the eastern coast Indians to this body of Mohegan invaders, who came down from the interior shortly before the arrival of the English. The division into two distinct tribes seems to have been accomplished by the secession of Uncas, who, in consequence of a dispute with Sassacus, afterward known as the great chief of the Pequot, withdrew into the interior with a small body of followers. This body retained the name of Mohegan, and through the diplomatic management of Uncas acquired such prominence that on the close of the Pequot war their claim to the greater part of the territory formerly subject to Sassacus was recognized by the colonial government. The real territory of the Pequot was a narrow strip of coast in New London county, extending from Niantic river to the Rhode Island boundary, comprising the present towns of New London, Groton, and Stonington."[1]

After the war ended, the Pequots were no longer a formidable threat to other Native American tribes or to European colonists who were establishing settlements along the coastline and farther into the interior of New England.

Author's photo of Fort Saybrook Monument Park, Old Saybrook, Connecticut. This photo was taken in July 2012.

Pequot strength was concentrated along the Pequot (now Thames) and Mystic Rivers in what is now southeastern Connecticut. Mystic, or Missituk, was the site of the major battle of the War. Under the leadership of Captain John Mason from Connecticut and Captain John Underhill from Massachusetts Bay Colony, English Puritan troops, with the help of Mohegan and Narragansett allies, burned the village and killed the estimated 400—700 Pequots inside. The battle turned the tide against the Pequots and broke the tribe's resistance. Many Pequots in other villages escaped and hid among other tribes, but most of them were eventually killed or captured and given as slaves to tribes friendly to the English. The English, supported by Uncas' Mohegans, pursued the remaining Pequot resistors until all were either killed or captured and enslaved. After the War, the colonists enslaved survivors and outlawed the name "Pequot."[2]

English soldiers, their Native American allies, and the Pequots all committed atrocities during The Pequot War. The destruction of the Pequot Fort in Mystic was a particularly bloody and brutal episode. Victims in this conflict were not just English soldiers and Native American warriors; women and children were killed when the places they called home became battlegrounds. Archival research provided an in-depth overview of this war and my ancestors' participation. The documentary film *Mystic Voices: The Story of the Pequot War*[3] provided a visual portrayal of how my ancestor Captain John Underhill dressed and spoke.

Visiting locations that played a central role in this war also helped me visualize the events from 375 years ago. One location central to this war was Fort Saybrook in present-day Old Saybrook, Connecticut. This fort was both a defensive stronghold and a home to colonists. Its construction was due to events transpiring in the early 1630s in England.

In 1631 the Earl of Warwick, president of the Council for New England, signed a unique deed of conveyance, called the Warwick Patent, to 11 of his closest friends and/or relatives, including the Viscount Saye and Sele and Lord Brook. A year or so later, four more gentlemen became patentees, including Colonel George Fenwick. Saybrook Point was included in this patent that gave the 15 lords and gentlemen a vast segment of New England stretching from the Narragansett River along the coast line south to about Greenwich, and west from these two points to the Pacific Ocean. In 1635 the Warwick patentees commissioned John Winthrop Jr. as the first Governor of the Connecticut territory. In 1635 Winthrop, learning that the Dutch were planning to permanently occupy Saybrook Point, sent a small vessel with 20 men and orders to seize control of the Point. Arriving on November 24, 1635 the Englishmen quickly put ashore with two cannons to ward off any attack by the Dutch or the Indians.[4]

Lieutenant Lion Gardiner designed and constructed the fort. He lived in the fort with his family, including his son David who was born soon after his parents arrived.

In 1633 the Warwick Patentees commissioned John Winthrop the younger as the "First Governor of the river Connecticut." Winthrop then engaged Lieutenant Lion Gardiner, a military engineer, for a period of four years to build a fort and lay out a town for the Warwick Patentees. Gardiner arrived in the bark *Batchelor* with his wife Mary in March of 1636 and began to build a stout palisido fort and a windmill for grinding corn. This was established, thus Fort Saybrook became the first military fortification in southern New England and the first legal patentee plantation (colony) in the area now known as Connecticut. Viscount Saye & Seale and Lord Brooke, two of the Warwick Patentees, gave Say-brooke its name."[5]

Author's photo of the statue of Lieutenant Lion Gardiner erected in present-day Fort Saybrook Monument Park, Old Saybrook, Connecticut. The inscription on the statute reads "In memory of Lion Gardiner, Builder and Commander of Saybrook Fort, 1635-1639, Erected by the Gardiner Family, 1930." This photo was taken in July 2012.

The landscape where Fort Saybrook once stood has been greatly altered since its construction in the 1630s. The most significant changes to the landscape occurred in 1870 when the land where the fort once stood was leveled for use by the railroad.

Before launching the attack on the Pequot Fort in present-day Mystic, Connecticut, a group of soldiers, which included Captain John Underhill, visited the fort. Decades later, Lieutenant Lion Gardiner wrote a narrative about the war. He recalled his reaction to the arrival of Captain Underhill and fellow soldiers. "And suddenly after came Capt. Endecott, Capt. Turner, and Capt. Undrill [Underhill], with a company of soldiers well fitted, to Seabrook, and made that place their rendezvous or seat of war, and that to my great grief, for said I, you come hither to raise these wasps about my ears, and then you will take wing and flee away."[6] Gardiner had good reason to be concerned about the safety of his family and the other inhabitants in the fort, as well as their food supplies. "Frustrated by their loss of control over subject tribes to the English, the Pequot warriors constantly harassed the fort, butchered livestock, and burned storehouses and haystacks outside the palisades."[7]

Fort Saybrook no longer exists. The fort that Captain Underhill visited burned in 1647 and was replaced by a new fort. What did the fort look like in the seventeenth century? The following description, coupled with drawings on interpretive markers in Fort Saybrook Monument State Park, helped recreate the long vanished fort. Near the original site of Fort Saybrook now sits Fort Saybrook Monument Park.

> Saybrook Fort at the mouth of the Connecticut River is often thought of as a fort in the context of the "old west." [It's] true that there was an enclosed area on Saybrook Point, but the "fort" likely included the entire area of Saybrook Point with three sides protected by water and the land access at the "neck" of Saybrook Point being protected by a [palisade] wall. The term "fort," in those days, referred to a tract of land put in a defended position, whereas a "fortification" referred to a structure which fortifies or defends, often consisting of an elevation of earth with guns and other implements of warfare and supplemented with a [palisades]. The fort at Saybrook Point was actually a fort within another fort.[8]

I visited the park soon after the 375th anniversary of the attack on the Pequot fort. Looking out at the Connecticut River, I felt an ancestor-descendant affinity with Captain Underhill. The landscape had changed so much that I wondered if John would recognize it if he sailed toward where the fort once stood. There was a sharp juxtaposition between Memorial Day weekend crowds strolling around the park and boats sailing on the river, and the charged wartime atmosphere that awaited Captain Underhill when he arrived at Fort Saybrook almost four centuries ago.

Captain Underhill was one of several ancestors of mine who visited Fort Saybrook during the Pequot War. My ancestor Thomas Stanton also spent time at the fort as an interpreter. Thomas learned the Algonquian language after arriving in North America in the 1630s. He was able to communicate with Native Americans living in the area. During the Pequot War, Thomas found himself in a precarious situation near present-day Fairfield, Connecticut.

> It was during the Fairfield Swamp Battle on July 14, 1637 that Stanton nearly lost his life. He arranged a temporary cease fire and managed to negotiate the surrender of 200 non-combatant Indians under a guarantee of safe passage. After these people passed beyond Thomas's exposed, forward position, the 100 remaining Pequot warriors opened fire without warning and advanced toward him. He was rescued at the last moment by nearby colonial troops. Stanton was a delegate at the Treaty of Hartford ending the Pequot War in 1638 and, in 1643, was appointed Indian Interpreter for all of New England by the Commissioners of the United Colonies.[9]

Thomas was extremely lucky to escape the Fairfield Swamp Battle alive. Both Thomas Stanton and Captain Underhill survived the Pequot War, and after the war, Thomas married and settled in Hartford while John made his way back to his family in Boston.

In the summer of 1637 my ancestor Francis Wainwright was also fighting in the war. By the time his name was listed in town records as a soldier who fought in the Pequot War, he had made his home in Ipswich, Massachusetts for several years. On July 13, 1637, just one day before Thomas Stanton was nearly killed, Francis had his own run-in. Captain John Mason's work *A Brief History of the Pequot War* shared a detailed account of Francis's experience.

> A pretty sturdy youth of New Ipswich, going forth somewhat
> rashly to pursue the salvages, shot off his musket after them till
> all his powder and shot were spent; which they perceiving, re-
> assaulted him, thinking with their hatchets to have knocked him
> in the head: but he so bestirred himself with the stock of his
> piece, and after with the barrel, when that was broken, that he
> brought two of their heads to the army. His own desert, and the
> encouragement of others will not suffer him to be nameless. He
> is called Francis Wainwright, and came over servant with one
> Alexander Knight, that kept an inn in Chelmsford.[10]

These were brutal times, and because Francis survived, I am here
today. It was hard to read an account like this and to internalize the
reality of what took place.

At the annual meeting of The Denison Society, Denison Day,
held in September 2011, the speaker was Dr. Kevin McBride, director
of research at the Mashantucket Pequot Museum and Research Center.
One part of his lecture focused on the likelihood that as a young man
my ancestor, Captain George Denison, fought in the Pequot War.
Dr. McBride highlighted the fact that many of George's neighbors in
Mystic were veterans of the Pequot War. In the years following the
war, veterans, such as George's neighbor Captain John Gallup, settled
in Mystic, which was familiar territory as the veterans had fought the
Pequots there. Dr. McBride's theory is supported by the fact that George
settled in Mystic with his family in 1654.

seven

King Philip's War

In the late 1630s and 1640s, many of my ancestors started moving their families out of the the Massachusetts Bay Colony and into settlements in modern day Connecticut and Rhode Island. Connecticut was favorable because the Pequots no longer posed a threat. "At all events, from the hour of that carnage, Connecticut was secure. There could now be unguarded sleep in the long-harassed homes of the settlers. It might be hoped that civilization was assured of a permanent abode in New England."[1] From the 1640s to the early 1670s, settlers spent time raising families, establishing communities, joining churches, and tending homesteads and livestock.

By 1675, men who had fought in the Pequot War were grandfathers in their fifties and sixties. It had been thirty-eight years since many of them fought in the Pequot War. Now, war with Native Americans in New England was coming again. It was a fight for survival on both sides: a fight to preserve and protect settlements and ways of life for both Native Americans and colonists.

For most New Englanders, King Philip's War was a terrifying, bloody, and brutal time from June 1675 to August 1676. King Philip was the English name of Metacom who was the leader of the Wampanoag tribe. What came as a huge surprise to me was learning that King Philip's father was Massasoit, who had befriended the Pilgrims

Author's photo taken in March 2012 of The Great Swamp Fight Monument. The twenty-foot rough granite obelisk was erected in 1906 by the Rhode Island Chapter of the General Society of Colonial Wars. The Great Swamp Fight was a pivotal battle during King Philip's War. This battle took place near South Kingstown, Rhode Island on December 19, 1675.

Author's photos of the four granite markers, which surround The Great Swamp Fight Monument. The markers bear the names of New England colonies. The markers are inscribed with the following names-Massachusetts, Connecticut, Rhode Island, and Plymouth.

when they settled in Plymouth. King Philip, instigating a war, showed how relations between settlers and Native American tribes in New England deteriorated in the fifty-five years after the *Mayflower* landed.

During the war, King Philip's allies were the Narragansetts, Nipmucks, Abenaki, and Mohawk tribes. The tribes allied with the English were their former enemies, the Pequots and the Mohegans. For colonists living in settlements scattered around what is now the state of Maine, hostilities continued until 1678. "This horrible conflict brought terror to the whole frontier; more than a dozen towns were totally destroyed and a much larger number raided. It is said that one man of military age in every sixteen died in King Philip's War."[2]

My American history classes only briefly discussed this war, despite the death and widespread destruction that took place. The research and written works from twentieth- and twenty-first-century scholars brought the war to life by profiling people and places prominent in King Philip's War. To learn firsthand about this grisly conflict and its aftermath, I visited some places associated with the war, like Smith's Castle in Rhode Island.

During this war, women were actively involved in protecting their families. Reading accounts like this one of what happened to women and children defending themselves and their families while their husbands, sons, and fathers were off fighting elsewhere took my breath away. Take, for example, the dramatic and courageous case of one heroic woman who lived in what is now the state of New Hampshire:

> The first depredations of these Indians upon these Northeastern frontiers began in September, 1675, at Oyster River (now Durham, N.H.)…The house of Richard Tozer at Salmon Falls, wherein were fifteen women and children was attacked by two Indians, "Andrew" and "Hope-Hope," but was valiantly defended by a young woman, who held fast the door till all the others escaped, and till it was hewn in pieces by the Indians, who then entering, struck her down, leaving her for dead, while they followed the others; one of three years was killed, the other of seven was carried into capitivity, but afterward was returned. The brave girl who defended the house revived after the Indians left her, and escaped to her friends and was restored to perfect health; and it is to be regretted that Mr. Hubbard, who relates this, did not record the name of the

heroine, as he doubtless could have easily done.[3]

King Philip's War forever altered the lives of New England's inhabitants, both colonial and native. It was a brave new world that emerged from the carnage and the scorched ruins of villages and towns across New England. Eric B. Schultz and Michael J. Tougias, in their book *King Philip's War: The History and Legacy of America's Forgotten Conflict*, wrote,

> Between six hundred and eight hundred English died in battle during King Philip's War. Measured against a European population in New England of perhaps fifty-two thousand, this death rate was nearly twice that of the Civil War and more than seven times that of World War II. The English Crown sent Edmund Randolph to assess damages shortly after the war, and he reported that twelve hundred homes were burned, eight thousand head of cattle lost, and vast stores of foodstuffs destroyed. Thousands of survivors became wards of the state, prompting churches in England and Ireland to send relief ships to New England's aid...For all their suffering, the English fared well compared to New England's Native American peoples... Some of the most grisly executions were of native women and children desperately trying to flee the war or surrender. One account estimated that three thousand Native Americans were killed in battle. In a total population of about twenty thousand, this number is staggering.[4]

When I first started writing this book, I knew Captain George Denison and William Williams fought in King Philip's War. As my research progressed, a longer list of Connecticut ancestors emerged who had fought alongside theirs sons, brothers, fathers, cousins, and neighbors.

> Almost all of the able-bodied men of Stonington were engaged in the Indian wars of their time...No list or roll of the Stonington men who participated in the early Indian wars has been preserved. The nearest approach to which may be found in "a list of the English volunteers in the late Narragansett war," as prepared by a committee for that purpose in order to secure a

Author's photo of memorial plaque erected in memory of Captain John Gallup, who was killed on December 19, 1675 during the Great Swamp Fight. John and his family had a farm in Mystic, Connecticut. His farm bordered the farm of Captain George Denison. This plaque was erected on the historic grounds of Smith's Castle in Wickford, Rhode Island.

grant of land for their services, as follows: **Capt. George Denison**, **Sergt. John Frink**, **Capt. John Stanton**, Capt. Samuel Mason, Rev. James Noyes, **Lieut. Thomas Miner**, Samuel Youmans, John Fish, George Denison Jr., William Denison, Nathaniel Beebe, Henry Stevens, Edmund Fanning, Thomas Fanning, John Bennett, William Bennett, Ezekiel Main, William Wheeler, **Gershom Palmer**, Samuel Stanton, Daniel Stanton, Manasseth Miner, Joseph Stanton, James York, Henry Bennett, Capt. James Pendleton, Robert Holmes, Thomas Bell, Henry Elliott, **Isaac Wheeler**, John Gallup, **Nathaniel Chesebrough**, **Ephraim Miner**, **Joseph Miner**, Samuel Miner, John Ashcroft, Edmund Fanning Jr., John Denison, William Billings, and Samuel Fish.[5]

Author's photo of the front of Smith's Castle. The earliest part of the home was built by Richard Smith, Jr. in 1678. 1,000 troops from the colonies of Massachusetts, Connecticut, and Plymouth gathered together at Smith's Castle before launching their attack on the Narragansett fort in the Great Swamp, which was located twelve miles from the house. The home's name is thought to come from the fact that the house on this site in December 1675 was fortified making it the castle of the Smith family. Richard Smith Jr. was forced to rebuild his home after it was burned by Native Americans in 1676 as a reprisal for the Great Swamp Fight.

The names in bold are ancestors of mine. These men shared many close connections established through marriage and family ties and neighboring farms in Connecticut.

One of my ancestors who played a prominent part in the war was Captain George Denison. He led men in pursuit of Native Americans through fields, swamps, and forests. George coordinated militia drills and launched attacks from the palisades he built on his Mystic farm. While he was away fighting, his family and other local families could take shelter in the palisades. George "built his first house, a rough log house, on a rocky knoll overlooking the meadows. Forever cognizant of the possibility of Indian attacks, he surrounded this rude home with a stout stockade, enclosing a spring and a couple of acres of land, surrounded by ravines. The spot was undoubtedly selected, with the eye of a military leader, for the purpose of defense against Indians."[6] For the most part, in King Philip's War, residents of Connecticut's towns and villages did not endure the death toll and destruction suffered throughout other colonies in New England.

Recently, archaeological digs have been taking place on the property of the Denison Homestead. These digs were inspired by George's participation and by his stockade being an important military location during this war. "Dr. Kevin McBride, of The Pequot Museum, is conducting an ongoing archaeological dig searching for Capt. Denison's 1600's stockade and evidence of the 200 men who trained here in 1676 for service in King Phillip's War. [For the past few years] UCONN students [dug] on the home site as part of CT [Connecticut] State Open House Day held in June. Visitors [were permitted to] take part in the dig."[7]

When George fought in King Philip's War, he was a grandfather in his midfifties. This was not the first time he had been in fighting mode. He had a lot of military experience to share with his fellow soldiers. As a young man, it is likely that he fought in the Pequot War of 1637. After the death of his first wife Bridget (Thompson) Denison in 1643, he sailed for England and fought in the English Civil War. In 1644, George fought in the Battle of Marston Moor and was taken prisoner by Royalist troops, although he managed to escape. In 1645, he fought in the Battle of Naseby where he was wounded. In his youth he was "a Cromwellian soldier, and [now he was] Provost-Marshal of New London County forces in King Philip's War, in which the Narragansett and Wampanaug Indians were pursued and defeated."[8] In his role as a "commander-in-chief"[9] during King Philip's War, George trained troops and held drills and musters at "his house in Stonington...[which was] surrounded by a stockade fort, and he also had a stone fort within the stockade, as a protection against the Indians."[10] Sadly, George's stone fort and stockade no longer exist, and I wish they did so I could get a better understanding of his life in 1676. It is possible to visit the muster grounds on his Mystic property, which are below the Denison Homestead built by one of George's grandsons in 1717. The muster grounds' military past has recently been resurrected again during American Revolution reenactments featuring The Second Continental Light Dragoons.

One of the dramatic events during this war that George participated in was the capture of Canonchet, the last sachem [chief] of

Author's photo of the plaque erected to the forty colonial soldiers, who were killed in the Great Swamp Fight and buried on the grounds of Smith's Castle.

the Narragansetts. Canonchet's death came after months of brutal and bloody fighting, and after the Great Swamp Fight of December 1675, which colonists fought against Canonchet and the Narragansetts. The death of Canonchet has been called "one of the most touching tragedies in American history."[11] Canonchet's grisly execution occurred in the spring of 1676 in Stonington, Connecticut.

The author of the Old Indian Chronicle tells us that the Mohegans "and most of the English soldiers, declaring to the commanders their fear that the English should, upon conditions, release him, and that then he would (though the English might have peace with him) be very pernicious to those Indians that now assisted us;" it was determined to put him to death. When told his sentence was to die, he "liked it well that he should die before his heart was soft or he had spoken words unworthy of himself." They carried out the sentence at Anguilla, near Stonington, all the Indians being encouraged to inculpate themselves equally in his death and mutilation "the more firmly

Author's photos taken in October 2013 of "Chief Canonchet's statue" in Narragansett, Rhode Island. The markers highlighting "Chief Canonchet's" life and identifying the sculptor were placed on either side of the statue.

to engage the said Indians against the treacherous Narragansetts, whereby they are become most abominable to all the other Indians." The Pequots shot him; the Mohegans cut off his head and quartered his body, and the Niantics built a fire, burned his quarters and sent his head to the Council at Hartford as a token of love and fidelity (acknowledged April 8th). "This was the confusion of a damned wretch that had often opened his mouth to blaspheme the name of the living God, and those that made profession thereof." So perished Canonchet, the most romantic figure that we know among the New England Indians; the unfortunate son of a most unfortunate father, both worthy of a kinder fate. Young and impetuous, he lacked the farsighted craft and subtilty that distinguished Philip, but as a leader of men and a warrior, the younger man was the superior, and his death was a terrible blow to the Indian cause. His death was as honorable to him as its infliction, and the shameful mutilation of his body was disgraceful to his enemies. Something of his lofty and dignified character seems to have impressed itself upon the grudging minds of his foes, but it called up no corresponding chivalry of action.[12]

Reading about the manner of Canonchet's death in Stonington was not easy. Learning that George was a member of the military expedition who captured him and that Canonchet was executed in Stonington made the war more real than simply reading about it. His death in Stonington and George's participation in his capture brought the war and the violence experienced by both native American and colonial families into focus again.

In August 1676, the war in southern New England (except in parts of present-day New Hampshire and Maine) came to an end with the killing of King Philip in Rhode Island. When the war ended and the tally of loss of life and destruction of property was taken, shocking information came to light. "This war caused by far the LARGEST per capita loss of life of any war involving Americans (native or immigrant). The total (Native American + English Colonial) per capita death rate in this SHORT war was about TWENTY times HIGHER than that of the US Civil War, the second worst American war by this measure."[13]

The fact that most Americans have never heard of this war is something that should be remedied. There are many lessons to be learned from this conflict, and the destruction and human toll resulting from this war is something that should never be forgotten. Legacies of King Philip's War continue to come to light in the twenty-first century due to the efforts of dedicated authors and historians. It is important that we remember this war, its key players, its devastating aftermath, and its place in American history.

Author's photo of the "Defenders of Fort Griswold, September 6, 1781" plaque at the gated entrance to Fort Griswold Battlefield State Park, Groton, Connecticut.

CHAPTER
eight

Fighting for the Fort: the Grisly History of Fort Griswold

On a beautiful clear day in October 1994, my mother and I set out from our home near Boston to look for traces of our ancestral roots in Groton, Connecticut. I was eager to work on the family-history assignment for my eighth-grade history class. At thirteen, I had no inkling this day trip to research family roots was going to set me on a course that would change my life. I was about to discover and wholeheartedly embrace the realm of genealogical research. Before we left the house, I gathered my supplies: camera prepped with a new roll of film, a notebook, several pens, and a huge road atlas. I also grabbed my historical guide, which was a photocopy of my Williams family line back to the 1660s in New London and Groton, Connecticut. My maternal great-grandmother, Forest (Kiester) Kuhns had compiled the lineage when she applied for membership in the Daughters of the American Revolution (DAR).

The emotions I experienced as my mother and I approached Groton recur whenever I do field work. I feel great anticipation at the prospect of new insights. My curiosity, excitement, and happiness pique when undertaking a new adventure. I feel a sense of amazement at how rich and colorful historical explorations can be.

Nearing Groton, my mother and I stopped for lunch to map out our research visit. We were not sure where to begin our search for

Present-day photo of The Groton Battle Monument. This granite obelisk was dedicated in 1830 in memory of the soldiers killed defending Fort Griswold during the Battle of Groton Heights on September 6, 1781. This photo is courtesy of Louisa Watrous.

family roots despite our preparations and guide book. After lunch we jumped in the car, thinking that we would figure out where to go first once we got to this coastal town. A sign on the horizon said "Welcome To Groton." We drove around until we stopped high above the Thames River looking across toward New London. We parked by a towering granite monument situated near the remains of a historic fort. This was the site of Fort Griswold where the brief yet bloody Battle of Groton Heights occurred on September 6, 1781.

> The Battle of Groton Heights holds the distinction of being the only major battle of the American Revolution to take place on Connecticut soil and was the last significant battle in New England in our war for independence from Great Britain. ... The Battle of Groton Heights occurred just six weeks before the British surrender at Yorktown, and historians believe this attack on New London and Groton was an attempt by the British Commander of all forces, General Sir Henry Clinton, to draw Washington's forces to the New London harbor area, thereby diverting his attention from attacking Cornwallis. To accomplish this, Clinton sent a fleet of 32 ships with a force of

more than 1,600 men to attack the two forts guarding each side of the Thames River: Fort Trumbull in New London and Fort Griswold in Groton. To lead this force was the infamous American traitor, Benedict Arnold. Arnold was well-aware of the forts, the topography, and the people here, since he was a native of Norwich, just a few miles up the river. Biographers of Arnold may differ on theories about his treason, but it's difficult to understand his actions of this day, which resulted in the burning of much of New London, and the massacre that occurred at Fort Griswold, so close to his native home.[1]

In the wake of the battle, many families in Groton and the greater New London area mourned the losses of brothers, husbands, and sons. After the battle, American and British casualty figures for the numbers of American soldiers killed differed.

The American version holds that after [Col. William] Ledyard gave up his sword in surrender, he was immediately killed with it and that a massacre ensued. Before the "massacre," it is claimed that less than ten Americans had been killed, but when it was over, more than eighty of the garrison lay dead and mutilated and more than half of the remainder were severely wounded. The British version makes no mention of the massacre or the manner of Ledyard's death. The entire battle had lasted only 40 minutes.[2]

A plaque on the Memorial Gate listed the "Defenders of Fort Griswold." There was a long list of the names of local men who were killed or wounded, and some who were later paroled; there were men who managed to survive the battle and were held captive on British prison ships. "The [American] non-fatal wounded numbering about 30 were marched toward the river bank to be imprisoned on a ship outside of New York: a fate maybe worse than death. 85 defenders lay dead on the fort or very near death, a handful escaped, and the rest already mentioned."[3] Sadly, the fate of some American soldiers was never ascertained. "Of those taken prisoner, many were never heard of again and assumed they died in transport on onboard prison ship."[4]

One name on Fort Griswold's defenders list revealed a tragic ancestral story. Captain Amos Stanton fought valiantly to the bitter end

The author standing in front of The Groton Battle Monument on September 6, 2013, which was the 232nd anniversary of the Battle of Groton Heights. Being photographed onsite on the actual anniversary of the battle meant a great deal to the author. Her ancestors, Captain Amos Stanton and Christopher Eldredge both fought in the battle and only Christopher survived.

to defend the fort. He is a maternal ancestor of mine and his untimely death during the massacre added a horrific new chapter to my family's narrative. "No one among the heroes that fell at Groton Heights, in military experience and ability, surpassed Captain AMOS STANTON. He had been in actual service in the cause of the Colonies almost from the commencement of hostilities with the mother country, and was an accomplished soldier. He had become distinguished not only as a military man but as a patriot, devoted to the interests of his country."[5]

Stanton was on leave when the fighting broke out.

> At the time of the battle and massacre at Fort Griswold [Amos] held the rank of captain in the Continental Army, and was home on a furlough. Hearing the alarm guns on the morning of the battle, he hastened to the fort, and was warmly welcomed by Ledyard and his brave compatriots. During the councils of war held by the officers of the fort on the morning of the 6th, he favored a different line of defence than the one adopted by his brother officers. His plan was to meet and skirmish with the British troops as soon after their landing as would bring them into the woodland near the shore. By skillfully manoeuvering his men, he could make his force appear far more formidable than it really was, and by skirmishing with the enemy and holding them in check, he would be joined by all the volunteers who were constantly arriving, some of whom refused to enter the fort, where, in case of defeat, there was no escape. But his opinions were overruled, and the result is known. The possession of great physical power and activity, with a firmness and courage that nothing could daunt, fitted him for a military leader. But what could personal prowess and superhuman strength do against an overwhelming disciplined force? Finding that the garrison were to be put to the sword, he rushed among the enemy and sold his life at a fearful cost, and finally sank to the earth riddled with bayonets and bullets.[6]

This ancestral connection to Fort Griswold was unanticipated. This discovery was much more tragic and dramatic than anything I expected to uncover. I was left with a newfound appreciation for Stanton's bravery in battle and his unwavering dedication to independence for the American Colonies. He was survived by a grieving widow and family including his widowed sister, Mrs. Prudence (Stanton) Fanning.

As we continued our exploration of Fort Griswold Battlefield State Park, my mother and I passed an older couple walking their dog. My mother approached them to see if they could help us with our local history inquiries. This courteous couple said that there was supposedly a tunnel running from under the fort to a nearby house built sometime during the Civil War. When my mother explained the purpose of our visit to Groton, the woman told us that down the hill from Fort Griswold there was a historic house once used as a hospital during the American Revolution. In the course of one day, the Ebenezer Avery House went from being a private residence to a makeshift hospital. It sheltered wounded and dying men, many of whom had been transported there in appalling conditions.

> After the Battle of Groton Heights on September 6, 1781, the wounded American soldiers were placed in a cart to be dragged down the steep hill to the shore of the river to be taken as prisoners in a British ship to New York. The wagon increased in speed as it descended the hill; the men pulling were obliged to let it roll. It got away from them and collided with a tree, causing much agony to the wounded occupants. They were taken into Ebenezer Avery's house and laid on the floor. And for many years, the bloodstains were plainly seen on the wide floorboards. The venerable house that stood for over two hundred years and more at the corner of Latham Street and Thames Street in Groton, CT, known to everyone on Groton Bank as the Ebenezer Avery House, the house where the wounded soldiers were taken after the Battle of Groton Heights.[7]

Christopher Eldredge was another ancestor who fought at Fort Griswold. He was born and raised in Kingstown, Rhode Island. His mother Mercy (Minor) Eldredge was a descendant of Thomas Minor who was one of the four founders of Stonington, Connecticut. By the 1740s, Christopher was in his late twenties and settled in Stonington where his neighbors included many cousins. His future wife was Mary "Molly" Hempstead, the granddaughter of Joshua Hempstead the Diarist. On Sunday, October 15, 1749, Joshua wrote in his diary, "Fair. Mr. [A]dams pr all day. Christopher Eldredge of Stonington & Mary Hempstead my Grandaughter & Samll Douglass & Mary Denison both of N.L. published."[8] Joshua's diary entry referred to Christopher and Molly's intention to marry being read from the pulpit on this particular Sunday along with another local New London couple. Two months later, on Wednesday, November 19, 1749, Joshua wrote, "Fair & cold. I was att home all day. toward night Christophr Eldrige & a company came (vizt) Jos Page Junr Shepard Wheeler [A]mariah Stanton & Hempstead Minor, Wealthy Whiting & a young woman Daughter of

Capt Joseph Hewit & Wee Sent for mr adams & my granddaughter Molly was Married to Christop Eldrege."[9]

After their marriage, Christopher and Molly continued to see Joshua Hempstead, as he was a frequent visitor to their home in the Wolf Neck District of Stonington. Joshua often referred to Christopher as "Citt" in his diary. Molly was lucky to have Joshua as a doting grandfather, as her father Nathaniel Hempstead died hours before her birth. In 1770, Christopher and Molly moved their family to a new home, which Christopher built in present-day Old Mystic. Their home on North Stonington Road still stands today as a private residence. It was in this house that they raised a large family, including a daughter Abigail Eldredge who moved into a home farther down North Stonington Road upon her marriage to Thomas Eldredge Williams. Thomas and his wife Abigail likely shared common Eldredge ancestors in the sixteen hundreds. Compiling the family tree of Thomas Eldredge Williams revealed that both his wife and his mother were named Abigail (Eldredge) Williams.

Christopher Eldredge survived the massacre at Fort Griswold. His name appeared on both the "Defenders of Fort Griswold Sept. 6, 1781" marker onsite at Fort Griswold and on the list of men wounded and paroled after the battle. He was "wounded in the face."[10] I wondered whether he was one of the wounded men taken to the Ebenezer Avery House after the battle. Two of his sons, Christopher Jr. and James, also fought in the American Revolution.

During the course of his long life, Christopher witnessed the brutality of war, suffered the losses of those closest to him, and experienced the joys of marriage, fatherhood, and being a grandfather. Sadly, in 1792 Christopher Jr. passed away, and his father Christopher sold the home he built on North Stonington Road, opting to move into his deceased son's smaller home in Old Mystic. In March 1811, eighty-nine-year-old Christopher died when he was digging a well. He was killed when the dirt walls caved in on him.[11]

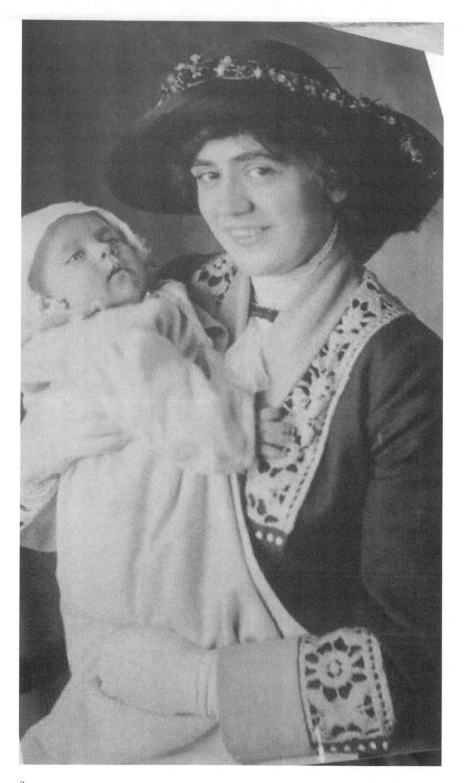

Revolutionary Love

On December 6, 1923, my great-grandmother Mrs. Forest (Kiester) Kuhns became a member of the Daughters of the American Revolution (DAR). The military service of her two maternal ancestors from Connecticut, Captain William Williams and Christopher Eldredge, made Forest eligible for DAR membership. Forest was a thirty-two-year-old mother of two boys when she joined the Jonathan Dayton Chapter in Dayton, Ohio. Forest's sons were eligible to join the Sons of the American Revolution through either their maternal or paternal ancestry. Her husband Robert Kuhns had an ancestor, George Kuhns, who also fought in the American Revolution.

Forest chose to document her line of descent from Captain William Williams of North Groton, Connecticut. Born on February 17, 1741, William was the fourth William Williams in his family line going back to his great-grandfather who had immigrated from Wales to New London, Connecticut, in the 1660s. William was born and raised on the farm established by his great-grandfather who had fought in King Philip's War. Having seen no portrait of William or his forebearers, I looked at portraits of his grandchildren for clues to what he might have looked like. A portrait of William's grandson, Elias Hewitt Williams, depicted his light blue eyes and light brown hair. Photographs of William's granddaughter Prudence (Williams) Appelman showed she

The author's maternal great-grandmother, Mrs. Forest (Kiester) Kuhns and her eldest child, Robert W. Kuhns, Jr. in a photograph circa 1913/early 1914. Forest was 22 years old in this photograph and she was living with her family in Dayton, Ohio.

THE WILLIAMS COAT-OF-ARMS

A lion Rampant, argent, on a Sable field; armed and langu'd Gules, wreathed; Crest, a moor fowl, signifying law, or that our Ancestors were Lawyers.

"COGNIZANCE OF THE OCCASION"
The motto in Welsh means—"What God wills, will be."

shared her brother Elias's complexion. The Williams lineage and family information on Forest's DAR application inspired my own genealogical and historical research.

Forest's official DAR record contained detailed information about William and his service during the American Revolution.

"Probate Office Town of Groton, Conn. Records. Records of Connecticut men in the military + naval service during the War of the Revolution 1775–1783-Town Records (Page 451–458). Lieut. William Williams of Capt. Morgan's Co. entered Service Sept. 8, 1776. (Records (Page 448). They were called to New York and North River where they suffered greatly."

Our family legend says he was wounded in the knee at the Battle of White Plains:

"[Declared] incapacitated for duty, [he] was discharged [and] returned to his home in Groton, CT where he made powder with pestle and mortar."

[This item comes from the records in Washington, DC.]

"Lieut. Wm. Williams of Capt. Morgan's Co. 8th Conn. Regiment Militia entered service Sept. 8, 1776, discharged Nov. 17, 1776. He was given a commission as Lieut. of the Fourth Company or [train band] in the Town of Groton, Conn. in 1774 by the Capt. General of the Colony of Conn. under George the 3rd, King of Great Britain. In 1777 he was given a commission as Lieut. of the same company from the Capt. General of the State of Conn. and in 1781 he was given a commission as Captain."

William and his fellow inhabitants of the thirteen British colonies in America were subjects of King George III. In 1774, he started his military career with a commission as a lieutenant in a militia loyal to king and country. When the American Revolution started in 1775, William was an unmarried farmer, tilling the land of his forefathers. Within a year, William had taken up arms and was fighting. William ended his military service as a captain fighting for the establishment of a country with a president governing, not a monarch.

William's military service in the fall of 1776 and the family legend about his knee being wounded at the Battle of White Plains sparked my interest in this skirmish. The battle took place in present-day New York State on October 28, 1776. The leading general for the British was Major General Howe, and the general for the Americans was General George Washington. William and fellow members of the Continental Army "dressed as best they could. Increasingly, as the war progressed, regular infantry regiments of the Continental Army wore blue uniform coats, but the militia continued in rough clothing. Both sides were armed with muskets and guns."[1] The month before the battle was a busy one for both British and American soldiers in the greater Manhattan area.

> At the end of September 1776, Washington's army occupied the northern tip of Manhattan Island and the ground to the west of the Bronx River north of Kingsbridge. Howe, from his positions on the rest of Manhattan, determined to outflank the Americans with a landing at Throg's Neck to the East of the Bronx. The British landing on 12th October 1776 was held by Pennsylvania, New York, and Massachusetts troops, forcing the British to re-embark on their boats and land further up river at Pell's Point. Meanwhile, Washington withdrew his main army north to positions at White Plains on the east bank of the Bronx River, north of Yonkers. On the insistence of Congress, a substantial garrison was left at Fort Washington on northern Manhattan Island. Howe and his British and German troops followed Washington via New Rochelle and up the Bronx River.[2]

The time William spent serving in Capt. Morgan's Co. 8th Conn. Regiment Militia was possibly the first time he had spent away from his Connecticut farm. It also might have been the first time in his life that he left the borders of Connecticut. His world must have quickly expanded with his experiences as a member of the militia. The outcome of the Battle of White Plains, according to the website Britishbattles.com, was that, "The Americans were driven back but were enabled to draw off from the White Plain position and march into New Jersey while the British returned to Manhattan. Generally considered to have been a drawn battle. However the American garrison on Manhattan and in Fort Washington was left

Author's photo of the original headstone erected in memory of Prudence (Stanton) Williams wife of Captain William Williams. Prudence was buried beside her husband in the William Williams Cemetery in Ledyard, Connecticut.

to its fate."[3] This rendition of the battle's outcome sharply contrasted with the one presented on the website About.com, which stated that, "With the loss of Chatterton's Hill, Washington concluded that his position was untenable and elected to retreat to the north. While Howe had won a victory, he was unable to immediately follow up his success due to heavy rains the next day [and the next] few days. When the British advanced on November 1, they found the American lines empty. While a British victory, the Battle of White Plains cost them 42 killed and 182 wounded as opposed to only 28 killed and 126 wounded for the Americans."[4] William was one of the American soldiers wounded during the battle.

There were discrepancies regarding how many men were killed or wounded during the Battle of White Plains. The website Britishbattles.com listed the American numbers of 300 soldiers killed,

The author photographed at Smith's Castle with a replica flag from the American Revolution.

wounded, or captured as "speculative,"[5] and noted 313 British soldiers were killed or wounded. Two other sources, TheAmericanRevolution.org and About.com's Military History information concerning the Battle of White Plains, agreed that 28 American soldiers were killed and 126 American soldiers were wounded, versus 42 British soldiers killed and 182 wounded.[6]

The wound William sustained to his knee meant a swift end to his military service in 1776. Subjected to the most basic battlefield medical care, William was lucky that his wound did not warrant amputation of his leg. "Throughout the war, medical equipment, supplies, and drugs were in short supply. In addition, most regimental surgeons were not well trained, especially at the beginning of the war. Medical officers often set to work with only what they could carry in their pocket surgical kit and performed the only useful surgery they knew—amputation. Medical treatment facilities had to be moved as the army was fighting and retreating. The field medical treatment facility was often in some local house to which the wounded were carried, dragged, or limped into on their own."[7]

Wartime radically changed William's life. In 1775, he was a British subject, and by the revolution's end, he was a citizen of America, a fledging democracy. William's discharge from active duty in November 1776 and his return home to his farm in Groton, Connecticut ensured he survived the war. His family dynamics changed during wartime. In 1780, he was married and at home making powder, not on the battlefield or later killed during the massacre at Fort Griswold in 1781. In quick succession, he became a husband and father, as well as a stepfather to two daughters from his wife's first marriage. Not long after his marriage, William lost his brother-in-law Captain Amos Stanton during the massacre at Fort Griswold.

William's wife Prudence Stanton and her brother Captain Amos Stanton were raised in a part of North Groton, Connecticut called "Pumpkin Hill." Her parents Captain John Stanton and Prudence (Chesebrough) Stanton were first cousins. The close family relation did not deter the marriage. Prudence Chesebrough and John Stanton were married on February 27, 1737, just a day before her sixteenth birthday; John was twenty-two years old. After John's untimely death, his wife Prudence was left to raise their six children, including their daughter Prudence (my ancestor) who was just eight years old.

In 1771, Prudence was a teenager. She married her first husband, Roger Fanning, in Groton. The future looked rosy for the newlyweds. Roger set about "[learning] the trade of a shipwright. Afterward, he actively followed the sea and became a sea captain."[8] Having grown up with a seafaring father, Prudence was familiar with the life a sea captain's wife led. When the American Revolution started, Roger was swiftly given a maritime role.

[He] was appointed carpenter of the *Shark*, a row galley built at Norwich. Manned by a crew of fifty men including officers, she carried two cannon, a nine- and six-pounder, along with small arms, lances, poles, and other weapons of war. During 1776 the *Shark*, with two other galleys built in Connecticut, was ordered to New York City. Her first commander was Theophilus Stanton, but when ordered to active service, Capt. Roger Fanning was appointed to command...The *Shark* being captured by the British during the following summer [1778], Capt. Roger Fanning is supposed to have returned to Groton, where he died about April 1779.[9]

Roger's death left Prudence a young widow with her two young daughters, Freelove and Cassandra, to raise; however, Prudence was not a widow for long. She quickly caught the eye of her neighbor, Captain William Williams. William was well acquainted with Prudence and her family, including her brother Amos, as their families were neighbors in North Groton. "Capt. Amos Stanton, one of Col. Ledyard's volunteers... [was] born and lived on the hillside (Highlands Development) on the southwest corner of the Mashentucket Indian land, neighbor to William Williams, at Cider Hill."[10] William Williams, Esquire (father of Captain William Williams) was the Justice of the Peace who had officiated at both the marriages of Prudence Stanton and Roger Fanning on January 16, 1771[11], and the marriage of Amos Stanton and Thankful Billing on January 31, 1772.[12] In his role as local justice of the peace, William presided over marriages that took place in Groton, Connecticut from 1748–1784.[13]

Prudence and William were married on February 13th, 1780. He was thirty-nine, and she was twenty-six. William Williams, Senior, Justice of the Peace, solemnized their marriage. At the Ledyard Historical Society, I found a photocopy of the original marriage record. "New London [Co] Groton February the 13th 1780 William Williams and Prudence Fanning both of N. Groton were married by me Mr. William Williams, Justice of Peace."[14]

The year 1780 was a milestone in the life of Captain William Williams. In February, he married Prudence and became a stepfather to her daughters, Cassandra and Freelove Fanning. In October, William and Prudence's first child was born. "William, the Child of W^m & Prudence Williams was Born the 13th of October 1780-On Fryday in Evening in a son." Proud grandfather, William Williams, Esq. made this record of his grandson William's birth. This record of birth along with that of other children born to Prudence and William was on file at the Ledyard Historical Society. These records are photocopies of the original ones.

The following year, 1781, ended as an unhappy one. Tragedy struck the Williams-Stanton families on September 6, 1781, during the Battle of Groton Heights (also referred to as the Fort Griswold Massacre). During this battle, Prudence's brother Captain Amos Stanton was killed. In their publication, *September 6, 1781: North Groton's Story,* Carolyn Smith and Helen Vergason poignantly illustrated his death. "Capt. Amos Stanton, a man of almost gigantic stature and herculean strength, on seeing the slaughter continued after the surrender...seized a heavy musket by the muzzle, exclaiming, 'My God, must we die so!' Springing upon the west platform, he laid about him, nearly clearing it of the enemy before being brought down by a musket shot."[15] Amos was one of the many men killed who lived in North Groton. Prudence and her family probably gathered together with other families in their community to comfort each other.

In 1785, William Williams, Esq. recorded the birth of another grandson. "Erastus Was Born the Child of W^m and Prudence Williams on the 16th of September 1785 about 9 of clock afternoon a Friday night." With this simple record of birth, a new chapter was added to my family narrative. Erastus was a maternal ancestor of mine, and he was a fifth-generation member of his family to live at Cider Hill Farm. As the last Williams to own the property, he was born a citizen of the fledging democracy, America, which was governed by a president, not a monarch.

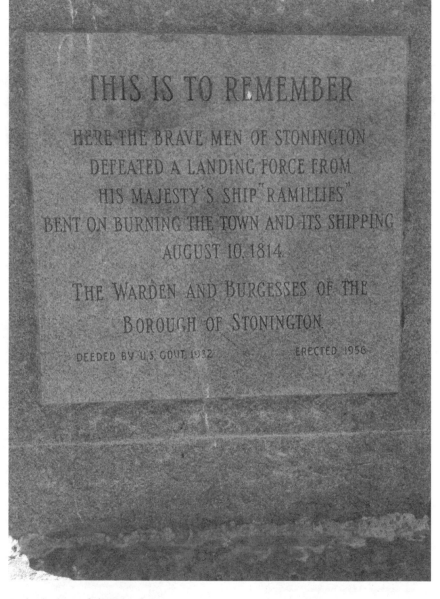

Author's photo of the War of 1812 monument in the Borough of Stonington, Connecticut. This monument was erected in memory of the local men, who defended Stonington during the British bombardment in August 1814.

ten

The War of 1812

Saturday, July 7ᵗʰ, 2012, was an idyllic summer night. I joined a steady stream of people strolling into the Fort Griswold State Park in Groton, Connecticut, for a fireworks display. It was not just fireworks that created a particularly festive atmosphere that night. The cities of New London and Groton were hosting tall ships as part of OpSail2012 events. OpSail2012 celebrated the two hundredth Anniversary of the War of 1812 and battles that took place locally in Stonington and Essex. Celebrations inspired a deep sense of pride about Connecticut's role in the war.

Opsail 2012 was my first visit to Fort Griswold State Park since 1994. The park was quickly filling with families laying out picnic blankets with bountiful spreads of sandwiches, desserts, and fruits. Children and dogs happily playing completed the summer scene.

Standing among the ruins of Fort Griswold, I experienced a collision of my family's narrative, past and present. Captain Amos Stanton and fellow patriots lost their lives here in 1781, fighting to realize the dream of an independent America. What was once a battlefield is now a public park and monument that my family helped to create, and we have not forgotten the legacy of their lives.

Captain Amos Stanton's early death meant he never met his nephew, Erastus Williams, born in 1785. Erastus grew up to become an American patriot like his father, Captain William Williams, and his maternal uncle, Captain Amos Stanton. His participation in the War of 1812 continued a family tradition of defending family, hearth, and homeland. Erastus was present during the Battle of Stonington and the British bombardment of this coastal Connecticut town in August 1814.

His participation in this battle provided a direct ancestral link to a time when America, still then a young nation, was forced to defend herself, again repelling British troops.

I felt immense pride the first time I beheld Erastus's headstone proudly marked with an American flag in the William Williams Cemetery on Town Farm Road. Knowing that Erastus's military service was honored and acknowledged made me happy. Visiting the William Williams Homestead in Ledyard, Connecticut, gave me a window into Erastus's world on the eve of the Battle of Stonington. All around me were tangible links to Erastus: doorways he walked through; rooms in which he slept; boards his feet crisscrossed as a baby taking hesitant steps, and later as a confident young man. These were thresholds he probably rushed over when he heard that British ships were sighted off the coast of Stonington. "For four days in August 1814, the tiny seaport of Stonington, Connecticut, was attacked by a large, heavily armed British naval squadron, intent on destroying it. Day after day, the village was bombarded with explosive shells, rockets, incendiary missiles, and cannonballs. All in all, at least fifty tons of British ammunition were thrown into the village. Stonington fought back against this massed armed might as best it could, but it was hopelessly outgunned…(To get an idea of the strength of the British squadron, its ordnance was ten times greater than the total of all of Andrew Jackson's artillery at the Battle of New Orleans)."[1] Despite the constant bombardment and having a smaller military force, the defenders of Stonington were ultimately successful in repelling the British naval forces.

What Erastus witnessed while Stonington was being bombarded by British artillery from August 9 to 14, 1814, was nothing short of impressive. Women, children, and sick or frail individuals who could not fight had been evacuated from the town. This evacuation helped save lives during the intense shelling that took place.

During the bombardment on the evening of the 9th, some bold spirits at Stonington took measures for opposing the landing of the enemy. The only ordnance in the place consisted of two 18, one 6, and one 4 pound cannon. They dragged the 6 and one 18 pounder down to the extreme point of the peninsula, cast up some breastworks, and placed them in battery there. The other 18-pounder was left in a slight battery on the southwest point, near where the present breakwater leaves the shore. By the streaming light of the rockets, they watched the approach of the enemy, reserving their fire until the barges and a launch came in a line near the southeast point of the peninsula, when they opened upon them with serious effect. The guns, loaded with solid balls, were double-shotted, and these so shattered the enemy's vessels that the little flotilla retreated in confusion towards the larger warriors.[2]

Erastus and fellow American soldiers would have watched the British ships being illuminated by the light of the rockets against the night sky. This would have been Erastus's first wartime experience, since he was born after the American Revolution. He must have been awed by the powerful munitions the British controlled. Amazingly, there were no American fatalities during the bombardment. Erastus's distant cousin from Stonington, nineteen-year-old Frederick Denison, was wounded in the knee, and after several agonizing months, he passed away on November 1, 1814.

In the years to come, Erastus could tell his children with great pride of the valor of the Americans who repelled British forces, despite great odds due to fewer troops and far fewer munitions.

The repulse of the British at Stonington was one of the most gallant affairs of the war, and the spirit there shown by the few who conducted the defense caused Hardy and his commanders to avoid all farther attempts to capture or destroy Connecticut sea-port towns. The assailing squadron had about fifteen hundred men, while the number actually engaged in driving them away did not exceed twenty. It was computed that the British hurled no less than fifty tons of metal on to the little peninsula during the three days. The loss to the British was twenty lives, over fifty wounded, and the expenditure of ten thousand pounds sterling. The affair spread a feeling of joy throughout the whole country and the result was a deep mortification of British pride.[3]

Unlike Erastus Williams, Captain John Appelman was not born and raised in Connecticut. On March 14, 1784, he was born far away in Wolgast, a part of Swedish Pomerania. He was the fourth child of John Jacob Appelman and his first wife. John later recalled his father: "of his profession I have no definite knowledge farther than he spent his time in attending to offices of the Presbyterian Church of which he was a Member as well as all of our family."[4] John's career at sea, which he referred to as "a Mariners life,"[5] commenced when he was sixteen years old.

John's emigration from his homeland occurred after meeting Paul Burrows, a man from Mystic, Connecticut, while in Liverpool, England. The men formed a strong friendship, and Paul "became a successful shipmaster, but was lost with his brother George in the ill-fated brig *Jane Coates*, which he commanded."[6] Paul directly influenced John's choice to settle in Mystic. Paul's father, Captain Paul Burrows Senior, let John live in his Mystic home until he established a home of his own. When John arrived in New England between 1805 and 1806, he was a Swedish citizen. In 1815, his home city of Wolgast became part of the Prussian-ruled Province of Pomerania.

By the summer of 1812, John was settled in Mystic with his wife, Matilda (Noyes) Appelman, and their first child, John, who was born on March 26, 1812, a few months before the war started. John's participation in the War of 1812 was recounted in his obituary.

And here in conclusion we may mention an episode in Capt. Appelman's career which was familiar to all of his early friends. We refer to the part he took in the re-capture of the prize sloop *Fox*, a Mystic vessel which was returning, in command of Capt. Jesse Crary, in the spring of 1813, home from some southern port laden with a cargo of corn. She was a fast sailer, and the British knew it. The enemy therefore planned a successful surprise, capturing the *Fox* and cargo but releasing her crew. With this fast-sailing prize well manned, the British managed to capture twenty-seven sail of vessels, in the short space of two weeks. Meantime Crary was concocting a scheme to retake his vessel. With a picked crew of about thirty men, and provided with a privateer's commission, the sloop *Hero* set sail under Capt. Ambrose H. Burrows, with his brother, Paul, the friend and shipmate of Appelman, as sailing master, and with the latter acting as gunner's mate. Provided with a four-pounder, small arms and ammunition, she first convoyed several trading vessels into Newport, and then run off South of Block Island to find the object of the expedition. The *Fox* was then in command of Lieutenant Claxton of the Ramlies, and soon descried the *Hero*, unarmed as he supposed, and trying to escape. Claxton bore down upon him, but upon a near approach declined to overhaul the *Hero* whose true character he suppected [my guess is that this word was meant to be suspected]. Now it was Burrows's turn to give chase. As both vessels were built at Mystic by the same man, Capt. E. Packer, their sailing qualities were known to be about equal. The wind had now increased nearly to a gale, and Burrows proved the more reckless in carrying sail. The *Fox* had two brass pounders, but they were rendered useless by the Yankees keeping the lee in such a manner that the enemy could not bring them to bear. She could only use small arms, while Burrows used both small arms and her single four-pounder. The *Fox*, finding flight impracticable, now attempted to ware round so as to bring her guns to bear when the saucy American ran her bowsprit into the enemy's mainsail, and fired her little cannon, loaded in good part with broken junk bottles, which John Appelman had the credit of suggesting and of ramming home. It not only shattered the enemy's sails and cut his shrouds but scattered consternation and mutilation on deck. The *Hero*'s men, in the confusion caused by this lucky shot, rushed over the sides, and in less than thirty minutes, Claxton's flag was hauled down and the stars and stripes went up. The *Fox* was recovered. Capt. Appelman by his coolness and pluck contributed not a little to the success of the expedition.[7]

John Appelman's ingenuity in a precarious situation meant that a reunion between the *Fox* and her sister ship the *Hero* took place. After the war was over, he spent the majority of his life as a sea captain sailing in and out of Mystic, and some of his eleven children followed in his seafaring footsteps. He passed away on May 8, 1869, and was buried in a family plot beside his wife Matilda in the Elm Grove Cemetery. In a fitting tribute to a life spent on the water, his grave faces the Mystic River, and in the distance is the Gravel Street home built for them in 1837. Erastus Williams's participation in the war took place on land, whereas the wartime experiences of Captain John Appelman took place at sea. Both men observed the war from different vantage points, and reading about the settings where they fought gave me a greater appreciation for their service to their country.

Photograph of Elias Hewitt Williams (he was a brother of the author's ancestor William Williams). Elias was a judge and briefly a Supreme Court Justice in Iowa. This photograph was reproduced courtesy of the State Historical Society of Iowa-Montauk Historic Site Collection.

CHAPTER

eleven

Cider Hill Farm Homecoming

When I first reviewed my great-grandmother Forest K. Kuhns's application for *Daughters of the American Revolution*, I made the association between the town of Ledyard and my Williams ancestors. William Williams settled in New London around 1662 with his new wife Arabella (Thompson) Williams after emigrating from Great Britain. Whether William and Arabella knew each other previously in England is unknown. They were married in New London. Nothing about Arabella's family background came to light during my research. Their farm and the first dwelling they called home stayed in the Williams family for centuries. It was located in present-day Ledyard, Connecticut. For almost two centuries, the property was known as Cider Hill Farm. In 1836, the town of Ledyard was incorporated. The farm received a new name, The Town Farm, because a portion of the farm had been set aside as a place for the town's poor to reside. A special government report, *Paupers in Almshouses, 1904* yielded an overview of Connecticut poorhouses less than seventy years after a part of Cider Hill Farm was divided.

> Connecticut-The selectmen of each town are the overseers of the poor and must provide for the subsistence of all paupers belonging to the town, whether the paupers reside there or not, but the expense must be borne by the town in which the paupers have a settlement which is gained, in general, by residence in a town for four years without receiving poor aid. Paupers supported by the town must be cared for in the almshouse and not by contract, except that partial support may be given outside

Cider Hill Farm, which was home to the Williams family from the 1660s until the late 1840s. This photograph was reproduced courtesy of the Ledyard Historical Society, Ledyard, Connecticut.

almshouses. Each town may establish its own almshouse under the control of the selectmen, or towns may unite for the support of their paupers in an almshouse. The selectmen as overseers of the poor are required to keep accurate records of the paupers whether fully supported or only partly relieved, and make returns with a statement of cost to the state board of charities.[1]

After reviewing this history of paupers and related provisions, I wanted to know more about Cider Hill Farm. I wanted to know more about its history as a family farm before the transition.

My discovery in the stacks of the Connecticut Historical Society in Hartford late one afternoon in April 1995 prompted my first visit to Cider Hill Farm. Because Williams was a common last name, the chances of locating information about my family seemed slim. Accompanied by my father, we were directed to a particular spot in the stacks where we might find information. We made our way through the silent lofty halls of the Connecticut Historical Society. There was time to select and review only a few publications, but surprises lay in store. The last book my father took off the shelf was a genealogy of the Williams family. We were shocked to see a photograph of the historic house at Cider Hill

Farm as well as a map of the town of Ledyard, Connecticut noting the exact location of the house. My ancestors, William Williams Jr. and his son William Williams III built the earliest part of the house around 1725. My family gradually enlarged the house over the years, and a direct line of ancestors owned and occupied it until the 1850s.

My father and I left the Connecticut Historical Society and stepped out into the April evening feeling successful with our research but still hoping for more information. Finding the documentation on the Williams family and the house photo was a wonderful surprise. Our visit to the historical society showcased the importance of archival records as a source of primary historical and genealogical research.

After my father and I settled in at our hotel in Hartford, I was giddy with anticipation. Would we be able to find the Williams homestead captured in the picture? The map we found made it possible to locate the homestead's location. The next day my father and I drove along winding roads in Ledyard. There was so much to take in that morning. My first impressions of Ledyard were of rolling fields, many colonial-era homes, farms, and small cemeteries by the side of the road.

My father abruptly stopped the car in front of a white colonial house with a red front door. He said, "I think this could be *The House*." Barely remembering to breathe in my excitement, I pulled out the copy we made the night before of the photo of the house. We held it up, and it was a match. The shrubs and bushes provided a less stark appearance than the house in the photo.

Time had changed the landscape my ancestors knew. Cider Hill Farm no longer existed, but the old house was still standing. Most of the acreage that once encompassed the property had been sold and developed. Trees filled in land around the house that had once been open space farmed by generations of Williams. The house gave its name to the road, Town Farm Road, that passed in front of the property. Williams family members have not forgotten about their ancestral farm and its original name. A cousin in Mystic explained that throughout her childhood in the 1930s and 1940s, her father took her and her sister to visit the house. He always referred to the property as Cider Hill Farm.

To the casual passerby, the house presented itself as a well-maintained colonial dwelling in a small Connecticut town on a country road, like so many that dotted the New England landscape. No historic plaque hung on the exterior providing a builder's name or a date for construction. When my father and I pulled into the driveway, I noticed a long red shed behind the house and the foundation of what was once a larger barn. I had not dared to hope that I would locate an ancestral house, much less visit one. I thought if I was really lucky, I would visit a ruined foundation or cellar hole in the woods. My imagination would have to conjure up the dwelling that once stood there, but after 270 years, the house had managed to survive.

If I were to step inside the ancient spaces, what whispered stories might the walls share with me? Having newly learned about my Williams ancestors, I was now staring at their home. Hastily snapping pictures, I hoped we would not be asked to leave abruptly. My father did not share my concerns about being a nuisance to the homeowners. He walked up the driveway that ran behind the house and knocked on the back door. He chose to knock on the back door because our friends who owned colonial-era homes in the Boston area came and went this way.

Surprisingly, in a few moments' time, the back door opened. The kind face of an older man peered out at us. He stepped outside to greet us, followed by his wife. Dorothy and Robert Brown had owned the home since the 1950s. Hearing that we had come in search of Williams family roots, Robert said with great warmth, "We have Williams coming by here often. Why don't you come on in and see the place? It is, after all, part of your history." In the Ledyard Historical Society's archives, I later found a copy of a letter that reinforced the Browns' hospitality and their pride in their home and its history. In 1972 Dorothy Brown wrote, "Bob and I love our home. We treasure the spirit and labor that motivated the planning, building, and care of it. We feel privileged to be able to have it and carry a feeling of responsibility to live 'life at its very best' within its walls."[2] The Browns graciously welcomed us, perfect strangers, into their home.

As Dorothy took me on a tour through the house, I found myself holding my breath in case this visit was all a dream. I walked through rooms where my ancestors had once lived and worked; in these spaces, the rhythm of their daily lives took place. Over the centuries, meals were cooked and clothes sewn, tools were repaired on cold New England nights, husbands and wives started their married lives, babies were born, generations of family members lived under one roof, and the cycle of life came full circle when the deceased were laid out before burial. Dorothy shared wonderful stories about her own family heirlooms that filled the home. She proudly pointed out a sea captain's bed, which retained marks made when nailed down to the cabin floor of a ship to secure it while at sea.

Photograph of the author taken by her father during their first visit to Cider Hill Farm. The photo was taken inside the Williams Homestead in April 1995 when the Browns owned the house.

The Browns had retained colonial features of the house, such as an ancient fireplace. In front of the mantle, my father took the day's only picture of me. I beamed happily back at the camera; this snapshot recorded an unforgettable moment. At age fourteen, I had decided to be a writer when I grew up and to write about my Williams ancestors.

By the time of my second visit to Ledyard in August 2000, the house on Town Farm Road had new owners. I was a college sophomore about to declare history as my major. Change was in the air. My intention to write a book remained, but my primary focus was my history classes and British study abroad programs.

Before driving by Cider Hill Farm, I stopped by the Ledyard Historical Society to see if I could learn more about my Williams ancestors and their home. Large windows allowed sunshine to flood into the archives room, illuminating Ledyard's rich history. I got my first peek at a large collection of Williams family documents. There were copies of family Bibles, newspaper articles, and genealogical information donated by Williams family members.

Among the newspaper articles was "Aura of Misfortune Surrounding Old Farm Replaced By Feelings of Warmth and Love" from *The Day*, dated October 30, 1978. On the front page were several

Mrs. Nancy (Hewitt) Williams and her daughter, Sarah Louisa Williams. Nancy was the wife of Erastus Williams the last member of his family to own Cider Hill Farm. This photograph was taken sometime before September 21, 1850 when Sarah and her older brother John H. Williams both passed away unexpectedly. Sarah was 13 and John was 19 when they passed away. This photograph was shared with the author by the Okey family.

photographs: one showed Dorothy and Robert Brown standing behind two large wagon wheels with the house behind them; the second photo displayed an overgrown cemetery where the Williams were buried. Additional photos identified William Williams and Lydia Williams. This was the first time I had seen photos of Williams family members. I wondered if this William was my ancestor who died in 1860. Lydia was his sister who also grew up at Cider Hill Farm. Around the same time as Lydia's 1848 marriage to Walter R. Fish of Mystic, her mother Nancy (Hewitt) Williams sold the farm. Nancy had been widowed, so she chose to move to the Midwest to join some of her children. I read tales of the homestead being a stop on the Underground Railroad with a secret staircase to concel runaway slaves. One of my relatives recalled seeing the hidden staircase when she was a little girl in the 1930s.

Morton H. Thompson Sr., a prominent author, and his wife left Hollywood to start a new life on the East Coast in 1949. They purchased the historic Williams Homestead. While living there, Morton wrote his last book, *Not As A Stranger*. Soon after finishing the book, he suffered a fatal heart attack. He was fifty years old when he passed away on July 7, 1953. *Not As A Stranger* became a bestselling novel and a movie starring Frank Sinatra. Tragedy struck again just weeks after Morton's death when his widow took her own life in the house. "Unfortunately, Thompson's widow did not enjoy the fruits of his success either. State police said that she killed herself two weeks later at the house with a .44 caliber pistol in despondency over her husband's death...An entry hall, where Mrs. Thompson is said to have committed suicide, has what Mrs. Brown says is called a coffin door—built close to the ground and wide enough for easy entrance and exit with a coffin."[3] Learning that Mrs. Thompson committed suicide in the front entry hall gave the homestead's "coffin door" a morbid significance. I recalled walking through that very hall when Dorothy Brown gave me a tour.

The Browns became the new owners of the house after the untimely deaths of the Thompsons. They were not put off by tragic events at the homestead. According to the article in *The Day*, "The Browns wanted the place—despite its reputation, which was compounded by the number of men (including Thompson) who suffered heart attacks there."[4] Dorothy Brown did not shy away from touching upon her husband's health while living in the house. She said, "Wouldn't you know, it was two years later that Bob had his first heart attack in this house." Dorothy commented that her husband's "work schedule was rigorous and probably contributed more to the [heart] attack than any legend."[5]

Now the Williams Homestead is home again to farmers. Amanda Levine and her fiancé Dylan Williams have ushered in a new era at the Williams Homestead with their creation of Town Farm Organic L.L.C. They operate a Community Supported Agriculture (CSA) "operation where [they] offer shares of [the] crop for a fee paid prior to the growing season. [They offer] full shares, which means a member of the CSA would pick up their share of fresh organic produce on a scheduled weekly basis."[6] Amanda and Dylan's hard work and dedication is the realization of the dreams of younger farmers in twenty-first-century New England.

March 2013 brought new revelations about ancestral connections to the Williams Homestead. New London was the backdrop for information that came to light at the Shaw Mansion home of the New London County Historical Society. The society's archives protect Joshua Hempstead's diary, and shared Hempstead ancestry was revealed at the Shaw Mansion. During a reception for Michelle Marchetti Coughlin's book, *One Colonial Woman's World: The Life and Writings of Mehetabel Chandler Coit*, I spoke with Nancy Steenburg, president of the New London

County Historical Society, and Keli Levine. The three of us learned that we are distant cousins through our mutual ancestors, Joshua and Abigail (Bailey) Hempstead. What a pleasure to chat with newly discovered cousins with Joshua's diary housed close by in the archives and Mehetabel (Chandler) Coit's original diary on display. In the 1660s, Mehetabel was a New London neighbor of Joshua Hempstead. Knowing that his diary and hers were both in the Shaw Mansion added to the rich historical atmosphere.

As Nancy, Keli, and I chatted about our Connecticut family roots and historic homes in the greater New London area, a surprising fact emerged. Keli's family owned a historic property in Ledyard. Inquiring about the property, I was shocked to learn they owned the Williams Homestead. Keli and her family purchased the property in the 1990s. Keli's daughter Amanda and her fiancé Dylan established Town Farm Organic LLC and Town Farm CSA. What were the chances? Distant cousins owning the Williams Homestead and farming the property was delightful information. Keli has not yet uncovered her own Williams family ties to the house in Ledyard. This was one of the most unexpected and enjoyable family reunions to take place while writing and researching this book.

Around a slight bend in the road and just a minute's walk from the Williams Homestead on Town Farm Road is the William Williams cemetery. It is set back from the road and bordered by trees and shrubs, which shade the ancient gravestones. When I first visited the cemetery in August of 2000, it was not visible from the road. Tall weeds obstructed any view of the graves, and there was no accessible path. A guide published by the Ledyard Historical Society noted its location and burials, but it was hard to fathom that there could be any headstones beyond the dense and weed-choked roadside.

After wading through tall vegetation, to my surprise I saw a few headstones poking up among the weeds. Crouching down, it was possible to make out a few words on the taller headstones. I found the headstones of Captain William Williams and his wife Prudence (Stanton) Williams who were buried side by side. Their headstones appeared to be in reasonably good condition. I had no idea how many headstones were still standing.

I was disturbed that the whole area was so overgrown and the headstones barely visible. The cemetery's state of neglect seemed disrespectful, especially since men buried here were veterans of

Author's photo taken
in April 2011 of Bill
Clarke the caretaker
of the William Williams
Cemetery, Ledyard,
Connecticut. He is stand-
ing beside the grave of
Captain William Williams.

American wars. The first William Williams fought in King Philip's War,
Captain William Williams fought in the American Revolution, and
Erastus Williams fought in the War of 1812. If their headstones still
stood, I wanted them to be visible and marked by flags to recognize
their military service.

I wanted the cemetery to be cleaned up. The best course of
action appeared to be sending a letter to the Ledyard Historical Society.
A handwritten reply acknowledged my concerns and informed me that
what I had seen was the norm rather than the exception. Many small
family cemeteries in Ledyard also needed restoration and maintenance.
No system was in place to take care of every cemetery and burial ground
in the town. It was understandable that families moving away from
Ledyard in the nineteenth and twentieth centuries meant cemeteries were
abandoned with no long-term maintenance plan.

I was wracked with guilt over having no clear solution to remedy
the overgrown Williams cemetery. I felt that my ancestors deserved a
well-tended cemetery, and I was not able to provide it by myself. Being
a sophomore at Denison University meant that my visits home were few
and far between. I wished for time to do frequent clean-up and to find

a way to put in place a weed prevention plan. As the leaves changed into brilliant hues of autumn colors, classes and study abroad applications took priority. I put cemetery cleanup on the back burner when I learned I would be spending a semester studying abroad in London.

Nearly a decade passed before I visited the Williams Cemetery again. In May 2009, my mother came with me for her first visit. I had no idea what to expect. As we parked our car, the sounds of children playing and the roar of lawn mowers filled the air. Nervously, I approached the cemetery. I prepared myself for the worst, as the passage of time could not have been kind to the stones. Noticing a gap in the stone wall running along Town Farm Road, we stopped to see if it might reveal a preliminary glimpse of the cemetery.

The gap in the wall was the entrance to a grassy area stretching from Town Farm Road to the cemetery. The cemetery's current state stopped me in my tracks. A recently mowed grass path led up to it. A plaque identified it as the Wm. Williams Cemetery, and a fence now contained the headstones. Had I entered a parallel reality? It certainly felt like it. Gratitude filled me as I excitedly examined all of the headstones. I found additional ancestral headstones to read, along with what remained of the inscriptions for Captain William and his wife Prudence. Years of guilt about the cemetery's condition vanished as I knelt down beside each grave. I showed my mother the graves of Captain William who fought in the American Revolution and his son Erastus, who fought in the War of 1812.

The well-tended appearance of the cemetery was no accident. The transformation was the work of a local man, Bill Clarke, a member of Ledyard VFW Post 4608. As this VFW Post now maintains the cemetery, Bill has a role as the Williams Cemetery Chairman.[7] During my visit, I was pleased to see that American flags marked the headstones of Williams men who fought. One morning in April 2011, I happened to visit the cemetery while Bill was mowing. I thanked Bill for all he and Ledyard VFW Post 4608 had done to make this historic burial ground accessible and beautiful. As I was about to leave, Bill said, "I didn't think anyone ever came to visit the graves. I never find flowers left here." His words struck a cord with me. My visits to the cemetery were spontaneous, so I never had flowers in the car. On Mother's Day weekend of 2013, spring was in bloom when I took flowers to the graves of my ancestors. This was a visit when I celebrated the lives of Williams women. It was a special time to pay tribute to Prudence (Stanton) Williams and

Margaret (Cooke) Willliams, as it was Mother's Day weekend. Both of these women were wives and mothers living in Groton, Connecticut, during the American Revolution.

Sampler created by Prudence Anna Williams (later Mrs. Prudence Appelman) probably around 1830. At this time, she was living with her parents and siblings at Cider Hill Farm in Ledyard, Connecticut. Prudence was the sister of William Williams (maternal great-great-great-grandfather of the author). Courtesy of the Appelman family.

Photograph of the children of Anna Matilda (Appelman) and William Larrabee. This photograph was reproduced courtesy of the State Historical Society of Iowa-Montauk Historic Site Collection. Picture of the author featured on the front page of The Elgin Echo newspaper in April 2011. The author is standing in front of Montauk the home of Governor William Larrabee, his wife Anna Matilda (Appelman) Larrabee, and their children. The black silk jacket the author is wearing once belonged to her maternal great-great-grandmother, Matilda (Williams) Kiester.

twelve

Pictures Are Worth
a Thousand Words

Writing at my desk in Massachuestts, I realized there was a lack of context about my Williams ancestors' mid-nineteenth-century migrations from Ledyard and Mystic, Connecticut. They moved to new homes in Wisconsin and Iowa. In early 2011, I possessed only a few mementos to physically connect to this chapter of my family narrative. I had found a small picture taken in Fort Dodge, Iowa, of my great-great-grandmother Matilda Williams. The picture captured her in her late teens/early twenties. I also had her personal photo album with unlabeled pictures and her long black silk traveling coat. These belongings were wonderful, but I still wanted to know more.

I visited Iowa in hopes of learning about Matilda's life before her marriage and subsequent move to Ohio in 1886. Matilda was born in Mystic, Connecticut, in 1856, but was raised in Wisconsin and Iowa. She was the first Williams to grow up outside the borders of Connecticut since the sixteen hundreds. Her father William died unexpectedly when she was four years old, and her mother Mary Elizabeth remarried a few years later. Matilda grew up in a large family. She had one younger brother, William Erastus Williams, and half brothers and sisters from her mother's second marriage.

It was my first visit to Iowa, and I was not sure what to expect or if I would find any clues about her life. Clermont was a key destination on my Iowa itinerary. It was here my maternal ancestor Nancy (Hewitt) Williams spent the last years of her life after moving westward from Connecticut. Before her marriage, Matilda spent time here with her grandmother.

I decided to bring Matilda's fragile black silk coat as a talisman of good luck on my trip. Happily, Matilda's coat fit me perfectly the first time I tried it on. The black exterior was complimented by a light-beige silk inner lining and small front hooks. Having the coat professionally cleaned and restored by Museum Textile Services, I learned it was altered over the years, changing the original style. There was a sense of family continuity when I wore Matilda's coat. She used it, and then one or both of her daughters Edith and Forest updated and wore it. As fate would have it, Matilda's coat stole the spotlight in Clermont, Iowa, when I was pictured wearing it during my visit to Montauk. Montauk is the historic former home of Matilda's relatives, Governor William Larrabee and his wife Anna Matilda (Appelman) Larrabee.

Driving over the bridge fording the Turkey River that flows through Clermont, I made my way to the Larrabee Building to view the Clermont Historical Society's collections. One item provided a firsthand look at my nineteenth-century Williams ancestors. Browsing the collection, I came across a painting of a man with bright-blue eyes and a long beard. His blue eyes illuminated his face and offered a sharp contrast to his white shirt and black waistcoat and jacket.

Curious about his identity, I was astonished to read this was my maternal ancestor, Judge Elias Hewitt Williams. He was Matilda's paternal uncle, born and raised in Ledyard at Cider Hill Farm. I had never seen a portrait of any Williams ancestor, much less one in color.

The top two pictures are Captain G.A. Appelman and his wife Prudence Anna (Williams) Appelman. These photographs were reproduced courtesy of the State Historical Society of Iowa-Montauk Historic Site Collection. In the second row of pictures on the left is their daughter Mrs. Anna Matilda (Appelman) Larrabee. This image of her portrait was reproduced courtesy of the State Historical Society of Iowa-Montauk Historic Site Collection. In the second row of pictures on the right is Anna Matilda's first cousin and the author's maternal great-great-grandmother Matilda "Tillie" Williams (later Mrs. Matilda Kiester). Tillie's photograph was taken at a photography studio in Fort Dodge, Iowa probably in the 1870s when she was a teenager. A portrait of Tillie's husband (the author's maternal great-great-grandfather), Dr. William Henry Kiester is below her picture. Tillie and William were married in Independence, Iowa in December 1886.

Photograph of Gov. William Larrabee in front of the Ledyard Oak in Ledyard, Connecticut. This photograph was reproduced courtesy of the State Historical Society of Iowa-Montauk Historic Site Collection. The Ledyard Oak was featured on the town's seal. The tree was 400 years old when it died in 1969 and it was the second largest tree in Connecticut.

Circa 1908 photo of Gov. Larrabee standing in front of his childhood home in Ledyard, Connecticut. The house is the historic Nathan Lester House, which was built in 1793 and is currently owned by the Town of Ledyard. William's mother was Mrs. Hannah (Lester) Larrabee. The famous Ledyard Oak was on this property until its death in 1969. This photograph was reproduced courtesy of the State Historical Society of Iowa-Montauk Historic Site Collection. The portrait above is the one of Judge Elias Hewitt Williams that the author saw at the Clermont Historical Society, Clermont, Iowa. The image is reproduced with permission from the Clermont Historical Society.

For the first time, I gained an idea of what Matilda's father William might have looked like. William and his brother Elias could have shared similar hair color and facial features.

Matilda's photo album represented a piece of my family's "forgotten chapters." It was small and nondescript, with stiff inlays to hold the photos. The nameplate on the cover was inscribed "Tillie," the nickname given to her because many relatives were named Matilda. The album's sturdy pages were barely held together. The spine was lost long ago. I had to cradle the album gently to view the photographs; these were the forgotten faces from Matilda's youth. She had no reason to label the photos of friends and family in her own album, but I wished I knew who the people were in the photos. In the middle of the album, I found a well-dressed couple that I thought might be Anna Matilda and Governor William Larrabee. Matilda's family ties in Iowa grew more close-knit as I learned about the family connections. Anna Matilda was the first cousin of Matilda, because Prudence (Williams) Appelman was Anna Matilda's mother and Matilda's paternal aunt.

Anna Matilda Larrabee and some of her children attended Matilda's wedding to William Henry Kiester held in Independence, Iowa, in December, 1886. Knowing Anna Matilda went to the wedding made me curious about her. The Larrabees built their Clermont home, Montauk, in 1874, so Matilda would have visited with them on occasion before her marriage. Touring Montauk, I could imagine Matilda sitting down for dinner with her relatives or listening to a music recital in the stately rooms. The house looked as though the Larrabees had simply stepped out to take a carriage ride and would be back momentarily.

Having seen a picture of my ancestor Elias Hewitt Williams, I was excited to find a picture at Montauk of his sister Mrs. Prudence (Williams) Appelman. I had now seen portraits of two siblings of my ancestor, William Williams. First was the portrait of his brother Judge Elias, and second was the portrait of his sister, Prudence. Prudence had light eyes, dark hair pulled back from her face in a bun, and a soft, kind expression that communicated to me that we could have happily conversed over a cup of tea had our paths crossed a century or so ago. Going to Iowa illuminated people and places that Matilda had known in her youth and a chapter of my family history I had not known.

Page from the estate records of Captain Thomas Wheeler (maternal ancestor of the author) listing the slaves he owned at the time of his death. "Estate of Wheeler, Thomas, Town of Stonington, Date: 1756, NO: 5672," CSL Reel #1016/LDS #: 1025057, New London County Probate District Packets, 1675-1850-Wetherell-Wiley, Abraham, State Archives, Connecticut State Library, Hartford, Connecticut.

thirteen

Slavery in Connecticut

My views of slavery and New England history were recast while doing research for my book. I learned that Connecticut, Massachusetts, and Rhode Island legalized slavery before the mid-Atlantic colonies of Maryland and Virginia. Colonists in New England tried having indentured servants and Native Americans work for them, but indentured servants were free to leave after they had worked off a set period of servitude; Native Americans were highly susceptible to European diseases, and many fled when the opportunity arose. African slaves came to be favored over indentured servants and Native Americans. Douglas Harper, a historian, lecturer, and writer, offered an informative perspective about the legalization of slavery in the New England colonies.

The first official legal recognition of chattel slavery as a legal institution in British North America was in Massachusetts, in 1641, with the "Body of Liberties." Slavery was legalized in New Plymouth and Connecticut when it was incorporated into the Articles of the New England Confederation (1643). Rhode Island enacted a similar law in 1652. That means New England had formal, legal slavery a full generation before it was established in the South. Not until 1664 did Maryland declare that all blacks held in the colony, and all those imported in the future, would serve for life, as would their offspring. Virginia followed suit by the end of the decade. New York and New Jersey formalized legal slavery when they passed to English control in the 1660s. Pennsylvania, founded only in 1682, followed in

First page of Captain Thomas Wheeler's will. Thomas lived with his wife Mary (Minor) Wheeler and their family in Stonington, Connecticut. He passed away on October 23, 1755. Richard Anson Wheeler wrote in his book *History of the Town of Stonington* that Thomas "was one of the most prominent and wealthiest men in his day and generation." "Estate of Wheeler, Thomas, Town of Stonington, Date: 1756, NO: 5672," CSL Reel #1016/LDS #: 1025057, New London County Probate District Packets, 1675-1850-Wetherell-Wiley, Abraham, State Archives, Connecticut State Library, Hartford, Connecticut.

1700, with a law for regulation of servants and slaves. New England slaves numbered only about 1,000 in 1708, but that rose to more than 5,000 in 1730 and about 13,000 by 1750.[1]

Learning that Connecticut was one of the first colonies to legalize slavery was a surprise. The idea of slave-owning New Englanders, some of whom might have been ancestors of mine, was not something I had expected to uncover. I would have been better prepared for the startling revelations that I had slave-owning ancestors had my history class curriculums focused on slavery in New England. The presence of 13,000 slaves in New England around 1750 should have warranted discussions of the institution of slavery in New England. The knowledge that the Massachusetts Bay Colony legalized slavery in 1641, followed by Connecticut and Rhode Island, could have provided useful background information about the colonies my ancestors lived in.

By the beginning of the American Revolution, Connecticut was the New England colony that had the most slaves. "On the eve of the Revolution, Connecticut had the largest number of slaves (6,464) in New England. Jackson Turner Main, surveying Connecticut estate inventories, found that in 1700, one in 10 inventories included slaves, rising to one in 4 on the eve of the Revolution. Between 1756 and 1774, the proportion of slave to free in Connecticut increased by 40 percent. All the principal families of Norwich, Hartford, and New Haven were said to have one or two slaves. By 1774, half of all the ministers, lawyers, and public officials owned slaves, and a third of all the doctors."[2]

Primary research into the whereabouts of my ancestors on the eve of the American Revolution disclosed that the majority of them were living in New London County, Connecticut. This particular county was "the greatest slaveholding section of New England, with almost twice as many slaves as the most populous slave county in Massachusetts. New London was both an industrial center and the site of large slave-worked farms; with 2,036 slaves, it accounted for almost one-third of all the blacks in Connecticut. New London town itself, with 522 blacks and a white population of 5,366, led the state in number of slaves and percentage of black inhabitants."[3]

This general background about slavery in Connecticut and in particular, New London County, helped put in perspective my ancestors' ties to the institution of slavery. In eighteenth-century New London, Joshua Hempstead owned a slave named Adam Jackson for thirty years.

Joshua frequently referred to him in his diary, and Adam lived in the family home, interacting closely with generations of Hempsteads. Nearby in Stonington, members of the Denison and Stanton families owned an African slave named Venture who bought his freedom and that of his wife and children. "Ultimately, Venture was sold to Oliver Smith, a small-scale Stonington merchant, and they reached a deal whereby Venture earned the money to purchase his freedom through various kinds of work, including cutting vast amounts of cordwood. It was in honor of the one master who did not betray or cheat him that Venture adopted the surname 'Smith.'"[4]

Venture died a wealthy free man and a property owner; he was buried in the First Congregational Church's cemetery in East Haddam, Connecticut. What is remarkable about Venture is not only that he freed himself and his family from slavery but also that, "Out of almost 12 million African captives who embarked on the Middle Passage to the Americas, only about a dozen left behind firsthand accounts of their experiences. One of these was Venture Smith, whose *A Narrative of the Life and Adventures of Venture, a Native of Africa: But Resident above Sixty Years in the United States of America. Related by Himself* was published in New London, Connecticut in 1798."[5] Venture's detailed narrative has enabled modern-day scholars to locate where he was raised as the son of a king in Africa; then they accurately mapped out his life after he became a slave in New England and later his life as a free man.

The question arose in my mind as to what enabled individuals in Connecticut and in particular, residents of New London County, to own more slaves than other New England colonies? Douglas Harper's commentary about why Connecticut had more slaves by the advent of the American Revolution provided an overview of the society in which my ancestors lived. "But Connecticut's large slave population apparently was based in the middle class. More people had the opportunity to own slaves than in Massachusetts or Rhode Island, so more did so. The greater prosperity of Connecticut's inhabitants and their frugal and industrious habits were responsible for this situation. The wealth of the colony was also more equally distributed, with few extremes of riches or poverty."[6] This commentary from Harper proved to be useful when I reviewed wills and inventories of ancestors' estates after their deaths. Harper drew attention to the "frugal and industrious habits" that enabled individuals in Connecticut, including my ancestors, to buy and own slaves in the eighteenth century.

Reviewing the wills of seventeenth-and eighteenth-century

ancestors, I learned about ancestors, such as Captain Thomas Wheeler of Stonington, Connecticut. Thomas "was one of the most prominent and wealthiest men of the town in his day and generation."[7] He lived in New London County where a large majority of slave-owning families were concentrated. On December 11, 1755, an inventory of his estate was made. It noted that at the time of his death, Thomas was the proud owner of "1 silver snuff box," "1 silver hilted sword," "1 striped Banayan and Holland jacket and breeches," and "1 sealed gold ring."[8] At the end of the inventory was a list of his slaves. The inventory listed fifteen individuals—nine females and six males, including one Native American servant named Mary and two mulatto servants, Harry and Elizabeth. The inventory listed the individuals in the following manner.[9]

	£.	s.	d.
1 negro man named Quash	2	10	
1 old negro woman named Juno		16	8
1 negro man named Cab	41	14	4
1 negro man Ceazar	37	30	
1 negro man Cipeo	45	16	8
1 negro woman named Hager	37	10	
1 negro woman named Flora	31	13	
1 negro woman named Sarah	40		
1 negro woman named Jane	37	10	
1 negro woman named Cloe	37	10	
1 negro girl named Phillis	15		
1 negro boy named Pharaoh	8	8	
1 servant mulatto boy Harry	8	6	8
1 servant mulatto girl Elizabeth	5		
1 servant Indian woman Mary	1	13	4

The approximate values of his most valuable slaves were: Cipeo £45, Cab £41, Sarah £40, and at £37 were Ceazar, Hager, Jane, and Cloe. His servants Harry and Elizabeth were each valued at £8, and his Native American servant Mary was valued at £1. I wondered if the African slaves were born in New England or brought from Africa.

The appraisal for Thomas's entire estate was £12,669. Thomas's will—dated June 24, 1755, four months before his death in October 1755—was specific about the fate of each of his slaves and servants, who would go to live with his family members. Thomas gave his son

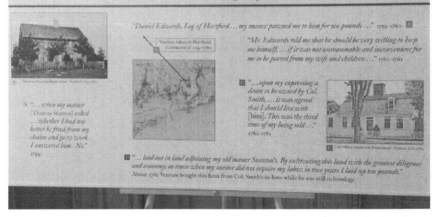

The author is pictured at the Connecticut State House in Hartford beside one of the panels used by the Documenting Venture Smith Project to illustrate Venture's life using his own words. Venture Smith was the son of an African king who was seized and taken from his home and sold into slavery in New England. In 1798 Venture's autobiography was recorded by Elisha Niles, a Connecticut schoolmaster and the narrative was published. The other panel shown here touches upon Venture's time as a slave in Stonington, Connecticut. Venture eventually bought his freedom and freedom for his family. He was a prominent citizen of Connecticut in the 18th and early 19th centuries. His inspiring life story was related in the book *Making Freedom: The Extraordinary Life of Venture Smith* by Chandler B. Saint and George A. Krimsky. These photos were used with permission from Chandler B. Saint.

Jeremiah (my next Wheeler ancestor in the family line) "one eighth part of all my lands and buildings. I also give him my negro man Sam, and my silver Tankard."[10]

The estate inventory valued the large silver tankard at £12 10s.[11] There was no mention in the inventory of a "negro man Sam." What had become of Sam between June 1755, when the will was dated, and December 1755, when the inventory of the estate was made? Did he die before December 1755? Sam was not the only slave missing from the inventory. "A negro girl Joanna"[12] who was to be given to Thomas's daughter Mehitable Babcock was also missing from the inventory.

My maternal great-great-uncle William Erastus Williams shared family stories about slaves with his wife in the 1930s. His wife typed out the stories he shared, and they were later placed on file at the Ledyard Historical Society in Ledyard, Connecticut. I shook my head in disbelief as I read his account of Cider Hill Farm's connections to slavery during the time the Williams family lived in North Groton, Connecticut.

> [The Williams] owned slaves. The family lived on one side of the house and slaves on the other. A door was cut through long after all the slaves were dead...As the slaves died, they had a little burying ground (private) for the whole family, black and white. They buried slaves in the same ground as white. One branch of the family was highly indignant at having their ancestors buried in the same ground as the slaves, and William Erastus Williams thinks that after the farm passed out of the family, this branch of the family went and dug up the remains of their family and reburied them in their own private cemetery.[13]

The family stories shared by William Erastus were the first account I found of my ancestors owning slaves. I was unprepared for the discovery that my ancestors owned slaves in Connecticut. This information had never been disclosed before by relatives. I was shocked to read about the likelihood that some of my Williams ancestors were reburied in a private cemetery sometime after Cider Hill Farm was sold out of the family. If this story is true, I hope to one day discover the area where the family's slaves were buried so their final resting places can be honored, too.

Author's photo: Nick Dimancescu and John "Whit" Davis at the Stanton-Davis Homestead, Stonington, Connecticut, June 2010.

The Stanton-Davis Homestead: Where Indian Law, English Law, and Slavery Intersected

I first visited the Stanton-Davis Homestead in Stonington, Connecticut, in late October 2009. I was immediately captivated by its historic appearance and curious about the stories housed within the ancient walls. No electric lights illuminated its rooms, no satellite dish marred the lines of the roof, and no huge television screen could be seen through the windows. "The Stanton-Davis Homestead is significant for the degree to which it is preserved. It is a simple, almost rough house, architecturally unrefined, [whose] heavy overhang, weathered siding, and primitive lines bespeak its great age. The house has been almost unaltered since the 18th century and is in need of considerable repair. However, the interior of this plain house is unexpectedly fine. The quality of the interior woodwork is completely belied by the roughness of the exterior but is outstanding and lavishly applied."[1] The homestead felt as though it belonged to a different century, an earlier time before modern technology and before all of the modern gadgets that fill my twenty-first-century life.

As I walked around the left side of the house, I suddenly came across a parked truck and an elderly gentleman. The homestead did not look occupied; I did not expect anyone to be there so late in the afternoon. I was worried he might reprimand me for walking around the property without invitation. There were no signs welcoming visitors to this historic homestead, which was in the process of being transformed

Author's photos: The author and her brother visiting the Stanton-Davis Homestead where they enjoyed an engaging tour given by John "Whit" Davis, June 2010.

from a private residence into a house museum.

The homestead was not yet a house museum open to the public. A personal family history blog shared that Whit Davis could be asked to give a private tour of the homestead. Whit had grown up in the homestead, which his family owned for generations. "Whit is a fountain of knowledge on local history and farming techniques, both past and present. He delivers amusing stories in his 'Swamp Yankee' twang, with a sparkle in his eye, and with great humor."[2] As fate would have it, the older gentleman standing by his truck was Whit Davis. He had stopped by the homestead to check on it. Whit and I struck up a friendly chat and quickly established shared family connections through our Stanton and Denison ancestry.

Whit offered to take me on a tour of the homestead, which was going through a transition from private residence to house museum. Two and half centuries of items were waiting to be catalogued and stored. Even the homestead's spacious attic was full and would have to be emptied and inventoried. Whit said at last count there were 150 chairs, for if a chair broke, it was moved into the attic rather than being thrown away. Whit's father John Lawrence Davis penned a thoughtful description of the house in his book, *The Davis Homestead: A Farm Since 1680 in Lower Pawcatuck, Connecticut.*

> The original stone chimney was torn down in 1754 and replaced with brick. The kitchen fireplace and the foundation were still in good condition, so they were left alone, but a new addition was added to the east end of the house with two more rooms downstairs and two more upstairs. Also, two more fireplaces were added. There were three "Christian" doors in the house (with a cross formed in the upper part of the panel), one of which is the front entry door. It still has its bronze knocker and butterfly hinges as of 300 years ago. The design of the paneling in the old part of the house is different from that in the new wing. The downstairs two front rooms have folding shutters at the windows and are paneled. Many of the doors have the old *L* and *H* hinges on them and are the original ones. On each end of the house are the original three-foot shingles laid twelve inches to the weather. They are still in good condition. The kitchen fireplace is fifty-seven inches high, seven feet seven inches long and two and a half feet from the backside to the hearth stone in front. The "Dutch Oven" is over three feet deep. There is a small smoke hole through the side of the oven that goes high up into the fireplace.[3]

The description of the homestead's rooms provided by John Lawrence Davis closely mirrored my first impressions of the historic spaces I toured with Whit. The homestead came to life through both Whit's colorful stories of his childhood and stories about the items we saw. He demonstrated how to use the original fireplace and Dutch oven. Women in centuries past wore long skirts and frequently had to reach to the back of fireplaces when cooking. It was easy for their skirts to drag too close to open flames or hot embers with tragic results. Whit told me that to figure out if the temperature was just right for baking, a cook would stick an elbow into the oven's front section. If her elbow burned, then baking could commence.

On a subsequent visit to the homestead with my brother Nick, we climbed the attic steps behind Whit to see where slaves once lived and to view the images they had made on the attic's walls. As we climbed the attic, Whit paused to point out a deep indentation in one of the steps. I felt a connection to the past as my fingers touched the ancient wood, well worn by feet from centuries past.

In the attic are amazing chalk drawings made by slaves who slept there during the first half of the eighteenth century. They appear on the rough wood beams that are part of the slanting roof. The slaves entered the attic through a separate entrance and stairway. We can only speculate about the drawings, but the sloop…is…a "Baltimore clipper," a two-masted topsail schooner, many of which were built for use in the trans-Atlantic slave trade. There are also representations of sawfish bills, and even a drawing of a woman in a long dress who appears to be pregnant. One hapless person kept a tally of some unknown event[s], perhaps the passage of days, or the amount of fish caught, using a series of straight lines.[4]

Seeing the ancient chalk images sent goosebumps down my spine. They looked freshly made, and I wondered about the individuals who had created the images. These pictures made centuries ago were a tangible record of slavery in New England, and the knowledge that these images were made by slaves made this horrific chapter of New England's often overlooked history come alive. Standing in the attic's dimly lit space as rain drops pounded the roof, I had to face the harsh truth of a dark part of my family narrative. Many of my ancestors and their extended family, including the Stantons who lived in this house, owned slaves. I knew nothing about the slaves my own ancestors owned and their life experiences in Stonington, Connecticut.

As we stood in the attic, Whit told us that this property is a place where English law, slavery, and Indian law all come together, given the home's long history: a history that encompassed slaves living in the homestead and earlier its initial construction by our common ancestor Thomas Stanton, who was a seventeenth-century interpreter between the colonists and Native Americans. One of the crops on Whit's land was Indian corn, the same type of corn traditionally grown by Native Americans. Whit shared his belief that, "Things should go back to where they came from." Whit practiced what he preached when he "gave some of his Davis corn seeds to the Native Indians that settled this area; the Mohegans, Pequots and Acquinasts (Wampanoags) of Martha's Vineyard."[5] He has distributed seeds to native tribes so that they can grow this crop again. Once Whit and his wife used this particular kind of corn to make 350 Johnny cakes that they took to the nearby Mohegan tribe a week before a Pow-Wow.

At the end of our tour, Whit said, "You never know who is going to drive in here." The Stanton-Davis Homestead attracts people from far and wide. They come to share their stories and take away new ones with an appreciation of the homestead's rich history. "The Stanton-Davis Homestead holds a unique place in American history as a touchstone for three different cultures: Native Indians, European colonists, and African slaves. Through the Stanton family in early Colonial New England, important representatives of these three peoples lived in or visited this house: chiefs of Indian tribes, most notably Uncas of the Mohegans; African slaves, including Venture Smith who bought his own freedom; and of course, the Stantons and the Davises themselves."[6]

Colonial Chroniclers

While searching for firsthand perspectives about daily life shared by New England ancestors, I discovered the diaries of Reverend Thomas Shepard, Joshua Hempstead II, and Thomas Minor. Thomas Minor and Thomas Shepard both emigrated from England to the Massachusetts Bay Colony. Thomas Minor arrived first in 1629, followed by Rev. Thomas Shepard and his family in 1635. Joshua Hempstead was the only diarist to be born and raised in the Colonies.

Their diaries collectively illuminate aspects of daily life, warfare, travel, farming, and religion in the seventeenth and eighteenth centuries. Shepard's diary was the earliest of the three. He penned entries from 1640—1644. He was a Puritan minister at the First Church in present-day Cambridge, Massachusetts. Shepard's parish was organized in 1636 after Reverend Thomas Hooker and his parishoners moved from Cambridge to Hartford, Connecticut. After the death of his first wife Margaret, Thomas married Reverend Hooker's daughter, Joanna Hooker. Before his death in 1649, Thomas married his third wife, Margaret Borodell, who was the sister-in-law of Captain George Denison. Thomas had connections to early Connecticut families through his marriages to both Joanna Hooker and Margaret Borodell, and his surviving sons followed in his footsteps to become ministers.

The year after his arrival in the Massachusetts Bay Colony, Reverend Thomas Shepard was preaching to his congregation and helping to establish Harvard College. "By order of the General Court of

Massachusetts, Harvard College was founded in 1636. A year later, because of the influence of Thomas Shepard, the college was located in Newtowne (Cambridge), where the students might profit by his evangelical preaching."[1] Thomas wrote diary entries, an autobiography, and religious works while residing in Cambridge with his family. His writings inspired Reverend Jonathan Edwards, especially *The Parable of the Ten Virgins*. Reverend Edwards was a pivotal New England minister in The Great Awakening, a religious revival movement that started in the 1730s. *The Parable of the Ten Virgins* was "a posthumous work, in folio, transcribed from [Thomas's] sermons, preached at his Lecture from June 1636 to May 1640; concerning which the venerable divines [William] Greenhil, [Edmund] Calamy, [Simeon] Ash, and [William] Taylor observed, 'That though a vein of serious, solid and hearty piety run through all this author's works; yet he hath reserved the best wine till the last.'"[2]

Thomas Minor started keeping his own diary in 1653 in Connecticut. His words helped to capture the experiences of his family and their neighbors during the first years of settlement in Stonington. Thomas, along with his father-in-law, Walter Palmer, was a founder of Stonington. As the years passed, he recorded marriages, his health and that of family members, planting tasks, community happenings, and military meetings and preparations during King Philip's War.

Joshua Hempstead II's diary transports a modern-day audience back into his world in early- to mid-eighteenth-century New London, Connecticut. The diary provided a rich chronicle of his life, information about business and commerce in the busy port city, and the lives of his family and fellow inhabitants of New London.

These diaries are rich personal time-capsules of early American history. The diarists acted as tour guides for the times and places they lived in. Their firsthand accounts shared the joys, hardships, and hopes they experienced. They recorded events and musings from their own lives and those of their families in the colonial American communities they called home.

Beginning of Reverend Thomas Shepard's *Journal*. The inside of the *Journal's* front cover has an inscription written by Rev. Ezra Stiles. "This book belongs to the Second Congregational Church Newport 1771. Given by Major Jonathan Otis Received by Ezra Stiles Pastor." Prior to the first entry Thomas recorded the births of his five sons on a flyleaf. On the other flyleaf he wrote, "This book I leave with my son Thomas Try all things and hold fast that which is good." Thomas Shepard's *Journal*. Manuscripts and Archives Division. The New York Public Library. Astor, Lenox, and Tilden Foundations.

sixteen

From Pulpit to Paper: Reverend Thomas Shepard and His Journal

T
he Reading Room at the New York Public Library was cool and quiet. Outside, New Yorkers and tourists alike were doing their best to stay calm in the intense summer heat. I had journeyed far from my home to view the original journal Reverend Thomas Shepard kept from November 25, 1640, to March 30, 1644. According to Michael McGiffert, the editor of *God's Plot: Puritan Spirituality in Thomas Shepard's Cambridge*, "The *Journal* lays bare the passion of a Puritan who labored to bring himself wholly into a right relation with the God Who not only imposed direction and pattern on outward events but also by His grace composed the discords of the troubled, sinning soul."[1] Thomas was born in Towcester, England, on November 5, 1605, and "according to the family record and tradition, he was born at the very hour when the Parliament was to have been blown up by gunpowder"[2] by the infamous Guy Fawkes and his comrades. Thomas was married three times; he was a graduate of the prestigious and ancient English bastion of higher learning, Cambridge University; he was a highly respected Puritan minister in Cambridge, Massachusetts; and he was a man of letters and strong religious convictions. He had three surviving sons, Thomas, Samuel, and Jeremiah, who all became ministers.

During his time as a student at Cambridge University in England, a particular event directed Thomas to a spiritual path that led

On the left-hand page is a note by Rev. Ezra Stiles. "Memo. By Ezra Stiles In 1747 the Rev. Tho. Prince of Boston printed this Diary from Nov. 25, 1640, to Dec. 27, 1641." Stiles was Congregational minister and seventh president of Yale College from 1778-1795. On the right-hand page is Thomas's first entry dated November 25, 1640. The first lines of the entry state, "November 25. I found my heart and mouth straitened on the lecture day and for want of enlargement much troubled. Hence I resolved to humble my soul before God, which the Lord helped me to do in this manner." Thomas Shepard *Journal*. Manuscripts and Archives Division. The New York Public Library. Astor, Lenox, and Tilden Foundations.

him to peace and acceptance by God.

As the fears which had been awakened by the solemn addresses of his pious friends gradually subsided, Shepard again associated with the loose and dissipated students of his own and of other colleges, and frequently joined them in their intemperate carousals, until, at length, upon a Saturday night, he drank so freely that he became grossly intoxicated and was carried, in a state of insensibility, to the chambers of a student of Christ's College...Filled with confusion and shame by the recollection of his "beastly carriage," he hurried away into the fields, and there hid himself, during the whole of that dreadful Sabbath, from every eye but God. The particular sin, however, which made him afraid, and drove him, like Adam, into concealment, not only awakened him to pungent sorrow for this act, but opened his eyes to see the exceeding sinfulness of his whole life, and the necessity of repentence for all his sins.[3]

Thomas was persecuted in England for his Puritanical views. He and his first wife Margaret (Touteville) Shepard and their young son Thomas left England to start a new life in New England.

His first parish was at Earles Cole, where he preached three-and-one-half years, receiving forty pounds yearly salary. His fame now attracted the attention of the church authorities (he being a non-Conformist), and December 30, 1630, was ordered to appear before Bishop Land in London, "closely catechized" and threatened with punishment unless he ceased his "heretical preaching." He preached privately, but was greatly persecuted, until August 10, 1635, when he sailed for America, having previously, in 1634, secretly and in disguise embarked for the same destination in a ship driven back by a storm and narrowly escaped wreck and death. After eleven weeks' passage in the ship *Defence*, he landed in Boston, October 3, 1635.[4]

Thomas was one of many Puritan ministers who left England due to religious persecution for their non-conformity with the Church of England. Thomas joined a circle of ministers settling in the Massachusetts Bay Colony. This group included Reverend Thomas Hooker; Reverend Richard Mather, who was the father of Reverend Increase Mather; and Reverend John Cotton, who was the grandfather of Reverend Cotton Mather. Knowing that other ministers had chosen to remove themselves and their families from England helped Thomas envision a new life in the Massachusetts Bay Colony, free from religious persecution. He settled with his family in present-day Cambridge, where he was a minister until his death in 1649.

Reading Thomas Shepard's journal, I realized how timeless, precious, and lasting the written word can be and how finding traces of the past in written form impart the most meaning to me as a writer. A Rare Book Division staff member carefully removed the journal from the archival box and carefully placed it on a special stand to support its the fragile spine and pages. A sense of belonging and continuity filled my mind; viewing his original journal provided a tangible link from the present day backward in time to Thomas's world. Two thoughts immediately crossed my mind—this was a possession owned and frequently handled by Thomas, and it was close to four hundred years old. *The Journal* measures "3 by 3 $^{3/4}$ and I $^{1/8}$ inches."[5] Thomas's small handwriting complemented the small size of the diary. I used a magnifying glass to examine Thomas's miniature sentences in black ink. His writing looked so clear and fresh that had I not known it was penned in the sixteen hundreds, I would have thought it was inked recently.

On the very first page, in Thomas's small clear handwriting, he recorded the birth dates for his five sons, three of whom survived to adulthood. The last birth recorded was the one I was the most eager to see. Thomas's fifth and last child, Jeremiah Shepard, was born on August 11, 1648, to his third wife Margaret (Borodell) Shepard. Jeremiah was a year old when his father passed away the following August at the age of forty-four. Following in the footsteps of his father Thomas and stepfather Reverend Jonathan Mitchell, Jeremiah become a minister.

Because Thomas's small handwriting proved challenging to decipher, even with the assistance of a magnifying glass, I consulted a reprinted nineteenth-century source to read excerpts from his journal. One of the entries described his frame of mind just a few weeks before the birth of his son Samuel. On October 9, 1641, he wrote, "On Saturday morning I was much affected for my life; that I might live still to seek, that so I might see God, and make known God before my death."[6] His message of making God known to his parishoners and feeling God's presence in his own was poignant. On October 18, 1641, Thomas wrote about Samuel's birth. His thoughts shed light on his relationship to God and the world.

> October 18. On Monday morning my child was born. And when my wife [Joanna (Hooker) Shepard] was in travail, the Lord made me pray that she might be delivered, and the child given in mercy, having had some sense of mercy the day before at the sacrament. But I began to think, What if it should not be so, and her pains be long, and the Lord remember my sin? And I began to imagine, and trouble my heart with fear of the worst. And I understood at that time that my child had been born, and my wife delivered in mercy already. Hereupon I saw the Lord's mercy, and my own folly to disquiet my heart with fear of what never shall be, and rather to submit to the Lord's will; and come what can come, be quiet there. When it was born, I was much affected, and my heart clave to the Lord, who gave it. And

thoughts came in that this was the beginning of more mercy for time to come. But I questioned, Will the Lord provide for it? And I saw that the Lord had made man (especially the church and their posterity) to great glory, to praise him, and hence would take care of him…And I saw God had blessings for all my children; and hence I turned them over to God."[7]

A magnifying glass greatly aided my study of Thomas's journal. It also symbolized the research I was doing. Primary research was allowing me to magnify the lives of my ancestors. Studying his handwriting, I noted how clean and deliberate his words appeared, in sharp contrast to my quick notes recorded in pencil. The journal made it possible to connect with Thomas in an intimate fashion. This journal was something he had handled, lived with, and used frequently. To be in its presence was a tangible way to feel I was in Thomas's presence, too. In an introduction to a book about Thomas titled *The Sincere Convert and The Sound Believer: With a Memoir of His Life and Character*, a view of his character was shared.

> Not inferior to Norton, Hooker, or Davenport, in intellectual strength and logical acuteness, he [Thomas] perhaps excelled them all in that fine, beautiful, practical spirit, which was at that time more needed than even genius, and in contemplating which, we become insensible to the greatness of his talents and the extent of his learnings. Although he was a prominent and an efficient actor in scenes of controversary and public disorder, which stirred up all the fountains of bitterness, such were his candor and tenderness that the odium of persecution was never attached to his memory; and while subject to like passions, and exposed to the same temptations, as other men, his reputation has descended to us without a blot from the hand of friend or foe.[8]

As I looked around me at the other occupants of the Reading Room, I noticed that I was the only scholar taking notes with a pencil. Everyone else had a laptop computer. I felt like an old-fashioned researcher when I sharpened my pencil, filling the silent room with the buzz of the sharpener.

The journal had its own journeys after Thomas's death in Cambridge. It became the possession of Thomas Shepard Jr., his eldest surviving son and namesake. Entries at the beginning and at the end of the journal record its arrival around 1771 in Newport, Rhode Island. Centuries after Thomas's death, his journal continued to offer a window into his thoughts and the daily ways that he fostered a closer spiritual connection to God. According to Randall C. Gleason,

> Shepard's autobiography and personal diary demonstrate how his major theological themes were worked out in his personal piety. In particular, Shepard's vivid account of his own spiritual awakening illustrates his belief that true conversion requires a total change of heart, mind, and affections. Shepard's journal also illustrates how the conversion of the heart that secures our union with Christ must be followed by a lifelong process of meditation to prepare us for our communion with Christ in Glory. Shepard's rigorous practice of self-examination during the height of his ministry in Cambridge, Massachusetts, may appear morbid to modern views of spiritual maturity. But Shepard took seriously Paul's admonition to "Examine yourselves to see whether you are living in the faith" (2 Cor. 13:5). His concern was not to foster religious despair, but his journal reveals how his daily self-examination and confession were meant to purge his soul of any hint of unbelief, sinful practices, or selfish motives that would hinder communion with God. Once his conscience was cleared, his affections for Christ were quickly rekindled through meditation on the wonder of his grace, goodness, and glory.[9]

When considering the wealth of religious thoughts and personal views that Thomas committed to the pages of his journal, the following statement made me appreciate how he enshrined his life and legacy in it. "Extracts from his diary, a book of choice thoughts, worthy to be the daily companion of every minister, show that with respect to his appropriate work he was diligent, and notwithstanding his outward trials, contented."[10]

Pictures taken by the author's father during their first visit in December 2010 to the final resting place of Rev. Jeremiah Shepard, his wife Mary (Wainwright) Shepard, and members of their family. Jeremiah and his family were buried in the Old Western Burial Ground in Lynn, Massachusetts where Jeremiah was a minister for many years. Jeremiah was the youngest son of Rev. Thomas Shepard and his mother was Thomas's third wife, Margaret (Borodell) Shepard. Jeremiah was just a year old when his father died in 1649. Mary (Wainwright) Shepard was the daughter of Pequot War veteran Francis Wainwright and his wife Phillipa Sewall. The burial site of Jeremiah's father Rev. Thomas Shepard is unknown. He was buried in Cambridge, Massachusetts after his death in August 1649. In these pictures the author is proudly pointing out the names of her ancestors carved into the ancient stone.

Page from the diary of Joshua Hempstead. Joshua Hempstead's journal, H378j 1711, Collection of the New London County Historical Society, New London, Connecticut.

CHAPTER
seventeen

New London's Native Son: Joshua Hempstead and His Diary

Joshua Hempstead kept a diary for almost fifty years. He wrote his first surviving entries in 1711 when he was thirty-three years old and the last entries in 1758 at eighty years old during the final year of his life. Joshua was born and raised in New London, Connecticut. His paternal grandfather, Robert Hempsted, emigrated from England and permanently settled in New London with his wife Joanna (Willey) Hempsted. They were part of a group of settlers who had the first house lots. Their oldest child Mary, born in 1647, was the first birth in the settlement to immigrant parents. Their only son Joshua raised a large family in a house he built on present-day Hempstead Street. Construction of the house took place in 1678, the same year his son Joshua II "the diarist" was born, in September. Joshua II was the only boy in a family of five older sisters and three younger sisters. His diary has given modern-day historians and general readers a detailed view of colonial life in eighteenth-century New London. Frances Manwaring Caulkins's book, *The History of New London, Connecticut. From The First Survey of the Coast in 1612 To 1852,* shared the following information about Joshua II's family and his diary:

> Joshua Hempstead, 2d—took an active part in the affairs of the town for a period of fifty years, reckoning from 1708. The "Hempstead Diary," repeatedly quoted in this history was a

private journal kept by him, from the year 1711 to his death in 1758. A portion of the manuscript has been lost, but the larger part is still preserved. Its contents are chiefly of a personal and domestic character, but it contains brief notices of town affairs and references to the public transactions of the country. Its author was a remarkable man—one that might serve to represent, or at least illustrate, the age, country, and society in which he lived. The diversity of his occupations marks a custom of the day: he was at once farmer, surveyor, house and ship carpenter, attorney, stone-cutter, sailor, and trader. He generally held three or four town offices; was justice of the peace, judge of probate, executor of various wills, overseer to widows, guardian to orphans, member of all committees, everybody's helper and adviser, and *cousin* to half of the community. Of the Winthrop family, he was a friend and confidential agent, managing their business concerns whenever the head of the family was absent.[1]

Joshua's diary was over 650 pages. "The diary was originally written on 12 by 7 1/2 inch unlined sheets, with the date slightly out to the left margin from the body of the day's entry, and frequently underlined. In the current edition, the dates are in bold type."[2] What motivated Joshua to keep a diary for almost fifty years? The reasons he chose to keep it were practical ones.

It would seem there were two paramount reasons. First, it was due to his natural tendency. The proclivity to jot down memoranda appeared at an early age, as may be noticed in his school books, some of which are still in existence. Secondly, it may be attributed to his need of a day book for entering the almost daily transactions of his various business employments, and one can readily see the value to him of such records. It is probable that the contents were not written for the public, for there is a certain frankness about them which would have been a matter of some embarrassment if published at that time.[3]

The diary's pages recorded both joyous and tragic moments in Joshua's life and the New London community. "By the time the surviving part of the diary begins in September of 1711, the

Hempsteads have six boys, ranging in age from twelve to almost two. Mr. Hempstead shows himself to be a flexible carpenter as well as a shipwright, making coffins, windows, a 'Cheast of Drawers,' and working on the new belfry. Sons Joshua and Nathanael were beginning to pull their weight and learn some carpentry."[4]

Joshua wrote three of the most poignant entries in the diary in August 1716 and July 1729. On July 30, 1716, Joshua's wife Abigail delivered their ninth child, Mary. There was a seventeen-year interval between her first child, Joshua Jr., and her last child, Mary. Abigail and baby Mary both survived the delivery. Sadly, this was an age of high infant and mother mortality rates. On Saturday, August 4, 1716, Joshua wrote,

> **Saturd 4** fair. I was in ye yard about Town al day. my wife very Ill. Mr Winthrop come to visit her in ye Evening used means for her Relief & Mr. Miller Let her blood in the foot about midnight. **Sund 5** [Sunday, August 5] fair. My Dear wife Died about half an hour before sunrise. I was at home al day except in the Evening I went to ye burying place. **Monday 6** fair most of ye foren. the body of my dear wife was buried about 2 Clock in ye aftern. it Rained Stiddy till late in ye night a Smart Storm...I carryed my babe [Mary] to Mary Trumans at night to nurse. **Tuesd 7** [Tuesday August 7] fair till night & yn Rain. I was down to Capt. Rogers's to get a Nurse for my Infant.[5]

Six days after Mary's birth, she and her eight siblings were motherless. Abigail was forty years old when she passed away. As was customary for this period, the majority of her life had been dedicated to her duties as a wife and mother; she spent almost twenty years of her life being pregnant and having children. In the midst of his grief, Joshua had to find a nurse for his newborn daughter. Joshua and his family soon suffered another heartbreaking loss.

> **Thursd 9** fair. I workt in ye yard in ye foren & in town in ye aftern. Joshua Is very Ill to day with a Sore Throat & fevar and Rachel hath been Ill 3 days with feaver & flux. Joshua was taken Extream bad about Midnight. I called Mr Jer Miller ye Schoolmaster & phyistion who Readyly gat up Came to See him & tarryed al night using Such Means as he thought most proper.

fryd 10 fair. my Dutyfull Son Joshua Died about Noon like a Lamb being 17 years & 20 days old a patren of patience. I was at home al day. **Saturd 11** fair. I was at home al day Except going to ye funerall of my dear Child who was Interred by his Mother about 2 or 3 of ye clock afternon.[6]

In a five day period, Joshua buried Abigail and their eldest child, Joshua Jr. Life in the Hempstead household had to carry on despite the heartache the family was suffering. In an age without modern medicine and expert medical care, death was a common visitor to colonial homes. Later diary entries revealed this was not the only double family loss to take place in a short period. In rapid succession, deaths and a birth occurred in Joshua's family in July 1729.

July 4 fryday. Thomas my dear & dutyful Son died about 4 in the Morning being Aged Twenty one years (Apr. ye 14.) Two months and Twenty days & buried the 5th day towards night. **Tuesday 8.** Fair & hot. I walked to the upper End of the Lot & back. my Eldest son Nathll [Nathaniel] who Lived with me Died about Ten of ye Clock at night. a Dear & Dutyful Son Ages 28 years 6 Months & 3 days: Leaving a Sorrowful Widow 2 Sons & She near her time againe: the 10th about 8 Clock at night She was dd of a Daughter. **Thursd 10** fair. I Rode up to the burial place to Order where to dig my Sons Grave. He was decently Interred about 7 Clock aftern. . . . **Sund 12** Mr Adam pr al day. a Sacramt Day. I was at Meeting tho. I went late. Son Nathlls Daughter Babtized Mary. She was Born within two hours after he was buried (vizt) 9 at night.[7]

These entries were sad to read, as Joshua lost two sons within days of each other. It was heartrending to learn that my ancestor Nathaniel Hempstead died so young, leaving behind his widow, Mary (Hallam) Hempstead and three children, including their daughter Mary, nicknamed "Molly" who was born right after his passing.

Reading Joshua's diary entries about the early death of his son Nathaniel caused me to wonder where he was buried. Research disclosed that he was laid to rest in the Antientest Burial Ground in New London, which dated back to the seventeenth century. It was here that Nathaniel's forefathers were buried.

Ye Antientest Burial Ground between Hempstead and Huntington Streets just outside of downtown New London was set aside for burial in 1652 and many of the early settlers, several of whom played important roles in this country's history, are interred there. Also in the cemetery are some of the oldest-known graves of early Black colonists. The town maintained it until 1793 and families owning plots continued to use it until 1845. As were many ancient cemeteries, this one was situated on a hill providing a scenic view for the resting souls. Benedict Arnold is said to have stood at this high elevation during the Revolution in 1781 to watch his British troops conquer Fort Griswold in Groton across the river and then burn New London.[8]

After his passing in 1758, Joshua was also buried in the Antientest Burial Ground. In the nineteenth century, the graves of Joshua, Abigail, and other Hempstead family members were moved to the Cedar Grove Cemetery in New London. Due to weathering and large patches of lichen covering much of the Connecticut sandstone headstone, the writing on Joshua and Abigail's headstone was not easy to decipher. I did not find a headstone for Nathaniel in the Cedar Grove Cemetery. The absence of his headstone indicated to me that he was not moved and reinterred in Cedar Grove, and that the Antientest Burial Ground remained his final resting place.

On July 22, 2011, an original section of Joshua's diary chronicling the years 1732-1750 went up for sale in an auction run by a Stamford, Connecticut, auction house. When the auction occurred, the New London County Historical Society already had most of the diary in its archives. The two sections of the diary were separated after a Hempstead descendant, Anna Hempstead Branch, asked for the section which covered the years 1732 to 1750 back after its transcription in 1901. "[Edward] Baker [executive director of the New London County Historical Society] believe[d] Branch intended to give the pages to the historical society when she died. But prior to her 1937 death, she suffered from dementia, he said, and her wishes were never conveyed. In 1941, Branch's first cousin, Henry Lyman, offered to sell the pages for about $600. The historical society offered him $25, but he declined. In today's dollars, Baker said $600 would have been the equivalent of about $9,000. Baker said he found out about the missing pages when the auction house called the historical society to authenticate the pages and be sure they were not stolen. He said he did not know the owner, who also had a number of old books that were auctioned off at the same time."[9] Happily, the New London County Historical Society became the proud owner of this section of Joshua's diary. It was reunited with the rest of the diary already held at the historical society.

I had an opportunity to view Joshua's complete diary at its home in New London as dusk blanketed the city one chilly afternoon in December 2011. Viewing the diary in the company of Edward Baker, the historical society's executive director, was a memorable experience. Seeing Joshua's handwriting and reading his original entries made him come alive. Joshua Hempstead's life and legacy continues to inspire historians, scholars, and colonial history enthusiasts.

Of all the ancestral homesteads that I have visited, Joshua's home in New London ranked as one of my all-time favorites. Each time I visited the Hempstead Houses, I was reminded of the seventeenth-century homes in Salem, Massachusetts, that captivated me from the time I was little with their distinct First Period architecture. The earliest section of Joshua's house was constructed in 1678 during the First Period in colonial American architecture. First Period homes were built between 1625 and 1725. "This style is easily recognized by such features as a second floor 'overhang,' a steeply-pitched roofline and lean-to additions, a prominent central chimney, and asymmetrical casement windows."[10] The circa-1678 house shares historic grounds with another house museum dwelling, the 1759 Nathaniel Hempsted House.

The 1678 Joshua Hempsted House "is a frame building and is one of New England's oldest and best-documented dwellings. Joshua Hempsted lived here his whole life, filling many roles, including farmer, judge, gravestone carver, shipwright, and father of nine children left motherless by his wife's death in 1716. As a boy, Joshua lived in the house with his parents and 7 sisters. As a young husband and father, he shared the house with Abigail and their 9 children. Later in life, he was joined by the enslaved African-American Adam Jackson, some of his children, hired helpers, and 2 grandsons whom he raised."[11] As for its architectural style, "The frame house reflects an English medieval style of building with its steeply pitched side gable roof, massive central chimney and diamond pane windows. A major addition was added in 1728 for Joshua's son Nathaniel and his family. It is more modern in style with different shingles and sash windows."[12] Nathaniel and his family briefly occupied the new addition before his death in 1729.

My mother and I received a warm welcome from the staff. During our first visit to the Hempsted Houses in September 2012, we learned Hempstead descendants frequently visit the houses. Discovering a huge Hempstead family tree hanging on the wall of the 1759 Nathaniel Hempsted House was memorable. The family tree made it easy for me to point out our ancestors' names to my mother, and to show her how we descend from the original immigrant ancestor, Robert Hempsted, who settled in New London in the seventeenth century. I noticed the spelling of Hempsted looked different than what I had seen before. Robert's last name was written Hempsted, not Hempstead. I discovered that later generations of Hempsteads added an "a" to the last name.

My mother and I left that afternoon with a copy of Joshua's diary we purchased in the gift shop, a greater appreciation for our Hempstead ancestry, and photos of us taken in front of the giant family tree in which we pointed out names of our ancestors. Visiting the Hempsted Houses was a highlight during my journey to trace my ancestral roots back to their starting points in early colonial America.

Picture of the author standing beside the grave of Abigail (Bailey) and Joshua Hempstead in Cedar Grove Cemetery, New London, Connecticut. Their graves along with those of some Hempstead family members were moved to this cemetery in the 19th Century from Ye Antientiest Burial Ground in New London. This picture was taken in July 2011 during a visit to Cedar Grove Cemetery with Hempsted Houses Site Historian Sally Ryan.

eighteen

Stonington Stories:
Thomas Minor and His Diary

Thomas Minor was born in the English village of Chew Magna, England, and he immigrated to New England in 1629. In 1634, Thomas married a fellow English settler in the Massachusetts Bay Colony, Grace Palmer, who had emigrated from England with her father, Walter Palmer, and siblings. Grace and Thomas had ten children; six lived to adulthood. Thomas became one of the four founders of Stonington, Connecticut, along with his father-in-law, Walter Palmer. The seventeenth-century wolf stones marking his burial and Walter's burial site can be found in Stonington's Wequetequock Burial Ground. Research into the origins and purpose of wolf stones revealed that colonists had "to place huge slabs of stone over the burial sites of loved ones to prevent wolves from digging up and scattering the remains."[1] Iva Arpin, a historian and cemetery researcher, "noted that wolf stones generally have end stones on either side, so when one looks down at them, they give the appearance of a bed."[2] The wolf stones marking the graves of Thomas and Walter stand out in the cemetery, as the majority of the headstones are upright stone markers.

From 1653 to 1684, Thomas wrote a diary that provided invaluable firsthand observations and information about daily life in

Page from the diary of Thomas Minor. Thomas Minor Diary-RG000 Classified Archives, 974.62 st. 7M, State Archives, Connecticut State Library. Image courtesy of the Connecticut State Library, Hartford, Connecticut.

Another page from the diary of Thomas Minor. Image courtesy of the Connecticut State Library, Hartford, Connecticut.

colonial Stonington. Thomas's diary and a diary kept by his son Manasseh Minor from 1696—1720 are now held in the archives of the Connecticut State Library in Hartford, Connecticut. In his diary, Thomas noted obstacles he faced as he worked to carve out a farm and homestead in the midst of the Connecticut wilderness. One of the concerns for his farm was the threat to his livestock posed by wolves. "The wild character of the country about his place may be seen from his frequent references to the loss of stock by wolves and the killing of deer. Indians were frequent visitors and often sought employment from him, payment being made in clothes."[3] Conversations with Palmer

Picture of Quiambaug Cove and former home site of Thomas and Grace (Palmer) Minor in Stonington, Connecticut. This picture appeared in the 1903 publication, *The Homes of Our Ancestors in Stonington, Conn.* by Grace Denison Wheeler.

cousins while writing my book revealed that Thomas, his wife Grace, and at least one of their sons, John, spoke Algonquian. Thomas and Grace would have thus been able to communicate with Native Americans living in the area around their farm in Stonington, Connecticut.

In December 2011, the world that Thomas wrote about for three decades became a real physical space for me. I drove along Cove Road in Mystic, past the location of Thomas's former home, which sat near the banks of Quiambaug Cove. This particular road caught my attention, not only because of its Minor family connections but also the spectacular views. Driving along Cove Road made for a eureka moment. I had tried to visualize Thomas's daily life and the land he farmed by reading his journal. Now I could peel back the layers of time by witnessing firsthand the landscape and water views where he once lived. I went home and reread his diary. Late into the night as I poured over the pages, his life and the lives of his family and neighbors were illuminated in new ways. I found myself daydreaming of walking alongside Thomas as he planted corn, plowed his fields, and traveled to New London, Boston, and to his neighbors' homes. The combination of his words and my visit to Cove Road reproduced strong visions of seventeenth-century Stonington.

I now appreciated Thomas's diary for its wealth of information about seventeenth-century Connecticut. He spent his days sowing peas, plowing fields, and entertaining family members and neighbors. He traveled to the Massachusetts Bay Colony and in particular, Boston,

Third page from diary of Thomas Minor. Image courtesy of the Connecticut State Library, Hartford, Connecticut.

frequently, making him more mobile than I expected. His diary revealed a hard-working family man who participated in his community and fought to defend his home and hearth when King Philip's War broke out. One of his entries, written in 1675 as the war raged, noted Thomas's active role in military preparations. He was a "Leeftenant" of the dragoons. Even as he attended military meetings, daily life had to continue on the homefront.

The ninth moneth is November and hath .30. days: Monday the first the third day I was ordayned Leeftenant of the dragoonors; and under pay for that service the Com'r's met at New London Monday the .8th Tusday the .9. the souldiers were apoynted to meet heare about 10. Or .12. oClock: the 10 day wee wer at Captayne Averies the 13 day saterday John Averie was heare it was wet: the 12. day of this moneth the Rames were brough from the Island Monday the .15. fryday the 19th I sent to Captayne Averie the News the 17th was a day of humilation: Monday .22. wee killed Two Cows: the .21. Captayne pembleton sayd that suckqunce would not deliver the captives: Monday .29. wee Looked Catle found fouer or five John Averie was married the .30. day Tusday I was at meshuntup we killed the swine.[5]

What was noticeably absent from this entry was what his wife Grace was doing while war raged and her husband was away fighting. I could not help but wonder what she was doing the November day her husband was appointmented "Leeftenant" of the dragoons" or the day that Thomas wrote that "Captayne pembleton sayd that suckqunce would not deliver the captives." Her thoughts on Thomas's participation in the dragoons and wartime life were not recorded by her husband. Entries such as this one offered a fascinating glimpse into Thomas's world and at the same time made me wonder about life on the home front for Grace and their children during King Philip's War.

One diary entry I was surprised to find concerned a dream that Thomas and his wife Grace both shared. In the midst of Thomas's many entries about planting, harvests, and his travels, this entry stood out because it touched upon an odd personal moment shared by the couple. "Agust 1662. I & my (wife) dreamed at one time my wife dreamed that I struck her & said that I strucke at a dogg & I dreamed that I was going by a red [author's note: No word was written here. This space was left blank.] which had a puppie and shee bit at me & I struck her & struck my wife in the face either with my hand or fist which waked my wife & shee waked me & asked me what I did doe."[4] This entry made me curious about what might have happened on this particular day in August 1662 to cause Thomas and Grace to share similar violent dreams. Turning to New Age dream journals for an interpretation of their dreams did not seem likely to yield thoughts on the cause(s) of their dreams. These dreams occurred at a point in Thomas and Grace's lives when they had been married for twenty-eight years and most of their married life had been spent raising children and working on their farm in Stonington. Did they have a huge argument and go to bed angry at each other? Why did Thomas record this dream in his diary? Did he mean to come back to this entry later to review it to find a deeper meaning or did he simply record it because it was such an out of the ordinary episode?

As I fell asleep nestled in a cocoon of comforters and pillows, my dreams were filled with Thomas and his sons plowing the fields and of a house full of children busy doing daily chores while watched over by their mother Grace. My admiration of Thomas's diary grew when his entries and the people, places, and events he mentioned transported me to the past.

LEFT and ABOVE: These pictures were taken by the author in Wequetequock Burial Ground, Stonington, Connecticut. A picture taken in December 2013 shows the wolf stone erected in memory of Lt. Thomas Minor. The author's brother, Nick is pictured in June 2010 standing beside the description carved on the Founders of Stonington, Connecticut Monument detailing the life of his maternal ancestor Lt. Thomas Minor. The author and her brother are descendants of the four founders of Stonington: Thomas Stanton, Thomas Minor, William Chesebrough, and Walter Palmer.

nineteen

As One Journey Ends, Others Begin

Tracing my family roots back to the *Mayflower* led to the discovery of forgotten parts of my family's history and has fostered my interest in early colonial American history. Studying maternal family lines ignited my hunger for the truth about my ancestors' lives and the times they lived in.

When I started researching my mother's family, I focused on the New England ancestry of my great-grandmother, Forest (Kiester) Kuhns. Her story of family roots started with the voyage of the *Mayflower* in 1620. A chance viewing of the documentary *Mystic Voices: The Story of the Pequot War* led to the startling discovery that seventeenth-century ancestors of my maternal grandparents, James and Faith (Colgan) Kuhns, knew each other. These ancestors became acquainted through early conversions to the Quaker faith, military expeditions in New England, and participation in civil and general colony affairs.

Exploring the lives of my ancestors and their times revealed the parts they played in the Pequot War, *The Flushing Remonstrance*, and King Philip's War. Primary research in libraries and archives, visits to historic homes and cemeteries, and discussions with historians about the settlement of New England brought the times and places my ancestors lived to life. Knowing who and where I come from on my maternal side has opened my eyes to the rich early chapters of America's past and to the individuals who helped shape New England, where I was born and raised.

A joyful part of learning and writing about my heritage is the enhanced sense of self and purpose that I gained from the experience. The more I learn about both the struggles and accomplishments that my ancestors faced, the greater my pride in who and where I come from. I also felt guilt and shame about the darker episodes of American history, which my ancestors played a part in, such as slavery and wars with Native Americans when many lives were lost. These negative feelings lingered until I started learning more about the societies and the beliefs that shaped my ancestors' views of their world. Living in the twenty-first century, I did not have to agree with my ancestors' decisions about wars, religious persecution, or slavery, but I did have to respect that they made choices in different times and in new settlements being carved out of the New England wilderness. My ancestors did what they felt was necessary to survive, or, in certain cases, to stand up for their beliefs in places and situations far removed from my own. Reading stories about my ancestors' successes, moments of heroism, misdemeanors, and exploits at times made me laugh, cry, and smile. I gained a new sense of strength and resilience as I learned what my ancestors endured, and if they could endure numerous struggles and hardships, then I, too, could carry on during upheavals and unexpected life events.

When I started researching my family roots in 1994, I thought it would lead to one project that shared my genealogical findings. Delving back into genealogical research years later has led to the insight that my research could produce more writing projects, and this idea inspires a wonderful sense of purpose. Until 2009, I had focused solely on Medieval English history and envisioned a career teaching and lecturing. A shift occurred when I started researching my own family roots. I wanted to know more about the people on the branches of my family tree and about their lives, marriages, families, and the events that shaped their community. In the blink of an eye, a decade of British history research moved forward in time to colonial American research.

A dream of mine from the beginning of my project has been to share my family's stories to inspire curiosity about forgotten chapters of American history. I highlighted the contributions of ordinary Americans who helped shape our nation's history in the hopes that I can inspire readers to find out who and where they come from. Researching family roots unlocks doors to the past and to the people and places that have shaped each of us. My hope is also that younger people can be inspired to take an active interest in their own roots and that they take advantage of moments with relatives to ask about their heritage.

"A Mapp of New England" (circa 1675) by John Seller. Map reproduction courtesy of the Norman B. Leventhal Map Center at the Boston Public Library, Boston, Massachusetts.

CHAPTER

twenty

POSTSCRIPT

Re-envisioning the 17th Century: Insights and Discussions about the Past

A uthor's Note: An earlier version of this piece appeared in the Fall 2013 Denison Homestead's *News Magazine*. This piece was inserted into the book after the indexing was completed. The information discussed here was not included in the index. This addition was necessary as new research insights were shared as this book was being readied for publication. There is a new resource which I am still reviewing that has a wealth of information to offer its readers. It is Dr. Lucianne Lavin's book, *Connecticut's Indigenous Peoples: What Archeology, History, and Oral Traditions Teach Us About Their Communities and Cultures* (copyright 2013).

On October 18th and 19th, 2013 the 17th Century Warfare, Diplomacy & Society in the American Northeast conference was held at the Mashantucket Pequot Museum & Research Center in Mashantucket, Connecticut. This was a two day event not to be missed! The conference got off to a great start with a welcome address by Dr. Kevin McBride and then an international group of academics started giving their 15 minute presentations. Presentation subjects ranged from "Re-evaluating the Causes of the Pequot War, or, the Pequot War was not an Indian War" to "Udder Destruction: The Role of the Dairy in the Creation of Conflicts between English Colonists and Native Americans in 17th

Century New England." Other presentations touched upon insights gained by studying 17th Century mirrors, the fate of children taken captive during the Pequot War and King Philip's War, and captivity narratives such as Mary Rowlandson written after her period of captivity during King Philip's War. It quickly became apparent that research from this dedicated team of scholars is changing what is known about 17th Century colonists and the Native Americans living in the Northeast. Many of the presentations made me reconsider what I knew about my maternal ancestors Captain George Denison and Captain John Underhill and their involvement in 17th Century Indian wars. Having the opportunity to speak with presenters over the span of two days was helpful as their comments inspired me to undertake new avenues of research.

The need to reconceptualize the changing nature of warfare in the 17th Century quickly became apparent. For example, John A. Strong in his presentation, "Wyandanch's Fun: Warfare and Diplomacy on the Long Island Frontier" made the point that in 1637 during the Pequot War a quiver of arrows was a symbol of authority and then on the eve of King Philip's War in 1675 guns had become the symbol of authority. Brian Carroll's presentation "Wampanoag Men, the Colonial Army, and Native Martial Culture in the late 17th Century: Benjamin Church's Indians Reconsidered" highlighted the participation of Wampanoag soldiers in the colonial military and how they were involved in attacks on French and native settlements under the direction of Benjamin Church. Carroll also emphasized the fact that King Philip's War was characterized by the destruction of both colonial and native villages and the killing of non-combatants.

David M. Powers an independent scholar gave a presentation on William Pynchon and Native Americans. Powers talked about his careful study of a deed dated July 15, 1636. He shared what he learned about Pynchon and his native neighbors in Springfield, Massachusetts. What Powers felt was conveyed by the deed's language was Pynchon's respect for Cuttonus the Native American leader from whom he bought an area called Agawam, which he renamed Springfield. Pynchon's respect for native customs, language, and the matriarchal society in which Cuttonus and his people lived was also reflected by the deed's language. Pynchon was on friendly terms with his Native American neighbors in the Springfield area and it was there that he operated successful business operations. Pynchon was a peaceful man who did not share the hostile views of Native Americans that so many of his neighbors harbored in the nearby Connecticut Colony. Learning about Pynchon's role as the founder of Springfield and his respectful interactions with Native Americans changed my views of early colonial settlement on what was the frontier of the Massachusetts Bay Colony.

This presentation in particular captured my attention because Pynchon's first years in the Massachusetts Bay Colony overlapped with the Denison family's first years in the colony. Pynchon and his family arrived in the Massachusetts Bay Colony in 1630 with the Winthrop Fleet and he helped Rev. John Eliot establish the First Church in Roxbury, Massachusetts. Eliot arrived in 1631 on the *Lyon,* which was also transporting the Denison family. George, his parents, and his brothers attended the First Church where they would have heard Rev. John Eliot preach to the congregation. The Denisons would have been acquainted with the Pynchon family given their church and community involvement. It is interesting to think of Captain George being tutored on the voyage from England by Eliot and then living in the same community as Pynchon. This presentation led me to wonder what impressions Eliot and Pynchon might have made on the adolescent mind of Captain George. How might have George's views of Native Americans been influenced by these men who respected and were respected by their native neighbors?

Comments made by Lisa Brooks from Amherst College during an engaging discussion focusing on "Wampanoag Historical Landscapes of the Seventeenth Century: Collaboration and Conversation" were ones that stuck in my mind. When studying the past and historic documents she reminded academics and independent scholars alike to consider the following question, "What do we really know? Her answer to this question was to "return to the evidence." What she meant is that it is necessary to ground one's ideas in the sources and one should not "claim to know it all" instead one should "listen to the sources" and above all else "return to the documents." She cautioned all of us to not fill in gaps with our own stories and to simply let historic documents reveal insights from the past. She also stressed the importance of reviewing sources such as Benjamin Church's narrative of King Philip's War side by side with other documentation.

One of the strengths of this conference was the focus on groups who are not always in the historical limelight-women and children. The plight of both colonial and native women and children in both the Pequot War and King Philip's War was discussed by presenters such as Jenny Hale Pulsipher from Brigham Young University. Pulsipher delivered an insightful presentation titled " Reexamining the Fate of Captives of the Pequot War: The Case of Ann Prask." She discussed the fate of young Ann who was taken captive during the Swamp Fight of 1637 in present-day Fairfield, Connecticut. Ann was five years old when she was taken to Roxbury, Massachusetts where she entered the household of the Hughes family. There were no slavery laws in the Massachusetts Bay Colony at the time of the Pequot War. Slavery laws were put into place a few years later in 1641 and these laws stated that slaves could include "captives of just wars" meaning Native American captives taken in Indian wars. Many Native Americans taken captive during the Pequot War escaped soon after capture or they later escaped from enforced slavery in New England. The fates of Native American captives sold into slavery in the West Indies is not known. What made Ann's story remarkable was that at the time of her death she was "virtually indistinguishable" from her colonial neighbors in Boston. Ann died in Boston in 1676 a widowed free woman who had owned property with her husband, John Wampus. Here again the question arose for me as to what impact the presence of Ann Prask might have had on Captain George. Ann lived with the Hughes family in Roxbury starting in 1637 at which point George would have been in his late teens and likely a veteran of the Pequot War. I wonder if George thought of her presence in his community. She was obviously quite young when she came to live in Roxbury so maybe her presence did not make a lasting impression in George's life.

In my mind, one of the most important points made during this two day conference was made by a Native American audience member, who reminded all of the assembled scholars to not forget that human beings were involved in the statistics they were carefully studying. The point being made was that so much of the study of 17th Century wars revolves around the facts-how many people were killed, how many soldiers fought in battles, how many captives were taken, and what percentage of a population was impacted by death and destruction in wartime. The human stories can often be overshadowed by statistics. This audience member went on to add that when Native Americans look at 17th Century history and historic documents concerning native peoples "it is family they are reading about." This point hit home. The descendants of many 17th Century New England Native American leaders were in the audience at this conference. The legacies of their ancestors live on in each of them and their family lines and oral histories have survived intact into the present day.

For those of us, who have Captain George as an ancestor, attending this conference was enlightening. We gained a broader perspective of the times that George and his family lived in and the colonial men and women who were both shaping and defending New England's fledgling communities. At the same time, we learned that many of George's neighbors in Stonington young and old-men and women-were able to speak Algonquian. Their linguistic skills would have developed as a result of the fact that they often had Native Americans working in their homes, they were fighting alongside them in wartime, and trading with them.

For me, this conference fostered a curiosity about many aspects of 17th Century warfare, beliefs, and native and colonial relationships. It has also inspired me to pursue further research into diverse aspects of 17th Century life. In the months and years to come we shall certainly benefit from the work of the scholars who presented. Their curiosity about the past enables all of us to gain new insights about the past.

Notes

CHAPTER ONE Discovering Denisons

1   Robert Charles Anderson, *The Great Migration Begins: Immigrants to New England 1620–1633*, Volume I, A–F (Boston, MA: New England Historic Genealogical Society, 1995), 522.

2   Anderson xxvii.

3   "Anne Bradstreet," 3 March 2013, <http://www.annebradstreet.com>.

4   Anderson 522

CHAPTER TWO "Why don't you speak for yourself, John?"

1   "Speak For Thyself Awards 2009," Alden House Historic Site, 19 October 2012, <http://www.alden.org/our_projects/speak09.html>.

2   "Alden's Duxbury Houses: John Alden & Priscilla Mullins Biography," Alden Kindred of America, 29 November 2011, <http://www.alden.org/our_family/aldenbiography.htm#Children>.

3   "Alden House History," Alden House Historic Site, 29 November 2011, <http://www.alden.org/our_house/househistory.htm>.

4   "Alden House History."

5   "Alden House Virtual Tour: The Great Room," Alden House Historic Site, 22 January 2012, <http://www.alden.org/Virtual%20Tour/tour.htm>.

6   Matthew Nadler, "Vermont man learns about his ancestors in Duxbury," Wicked Local Duxbury, 22 January 2012, <http://www.wickedlocal.com/duxbury/features/x1696237692/Vermont-man-learns-about-his-ancestors-in-Duxbury?zc_p=0#axzz2UW6hkxfw>.

7   "Vermont man learns about his ancestors in Duxbury."

8   "Vermont man learns about his ancestors in Duxbury."

9   "Vermont man learns about his ancestors in Duxbury."

10   "Alden House History."

11   "Five Generations Project," Alden Kindred of America, 22 January 2012, <http://www.alden.org/genealogy/documents/five-gen1.html#HISTORY>.

12   "John Alden & Priscilla Mullins Biography."

13 Esther Littleford Woodworth-Barnes, compiler, and Alicia Crane Williams, ed., *Mayflower Families Through Five Generations: Descendants of the Pilgrims Who Landed at Plymouth, Mass.,* December 1620, Family of John Alden, Vol. 16. 1 (Plymouth, MA: General Society of *Mayflower* Descendants, 1999), 167.

14 "The John Alden Broadside: Issued to Commemorate the 300th Anniversary of the death of John Alden," issued by Alden Kindred of America, Inc., Duxbury, MA, revised and reprinted 1989 and broadside image republished with permission of the Boston Athenaeum.

CHAPTER THREE Colonial Crimes and Punishments

1 "The Great Migration, A Survey of New England: 1620-1640," The Great Migration Study Project, 3 March 2013, <http://www.greatmigration.org>.

2 Robert Charles Anderson, *The Great Migration Begins: Immigrants to New England 1620– 1633,* Volume 1, A–F (Boston, MA: New England Historic Genealogical Society, 1995), 435.

3 Anderson 437.

4 Anderson 436.

5 Edgar J. McManus, *Law and Liberty in Early New England: Criminal Justice and Due Process,* 1620–1692 (Amherst, MA: University of Massachusetts Press, 1993), 49.

6 McManus 49.

7 Anderson 438.

8 McManus 165.

9 Anderson 438–439.

10 Anderson 436.

11 McManus 165.

12 McManus 165.

13 Anderson 435.

14 Anderson 436.

15 Anderson 436.

16 Anderson 218.

17 Anderson 217.

18 Anderson 217.

19 "Biography of Walter Palmer," Walter Palmer Society, 3 March 2013, <http://walterpalmer.com/Walter_Palmer_Bio.htm>.

20 Anderson 218.

21 "Biography of Walter Palmer"

22 "Biography of Walter Palmer."

23 "Biography of Walter Palmer."

CHAPTER FOUR Quakers in New England

1 "Mass Moments: Quakers Outlawed in Plymouth December 3, 1658," 17 February 2012, <http://www.massmoments.org/moment.cfm?mid=347>.

2 "The Freemen of the Massachusetts Bay Colony 1630–1636," The Winthrop Society, 18 February 2013, <http://www.winthropsociety.com/doc_freemen.php>.

3 "The Freemen of the Massachusetts Bay Colony 1630–1636."

4 Ruth Talbot Plimpton, *Mary Dyer: Biography of a Rebel Quaker* (Boston, MA: Branden Publishing Company, Inc., 1994), 23.

5 Roland Marchand, "The Antinomian Controversy (University)," The History Project— University of California, Davis, 17 February 2013, <http://historyproject.ucdavis.edu/lessons/view_lesson.php?id=8>.

6 Marchand.

7 "Anne Hutchinson and the Antinomian Controversy," 4 March 2013, <http://faculty.samford.edu/~whbunch/Case%202.pdf>.

8 Josephine C. Frost, ed., *Underhill Genealogy*, Vol. I (Privately published by Myron C. Taylor, 1932), 5.

9 Frost 5.

10 "Anne Hutchinson and John Wheelwright," 4 March 2013, <http://www.americanancestors.org/great-migration-newsletter-anne-hutchinson>.

11 Frost 8.

12 John M. Barry, *Roger Williams and The Creation of the American Soul: Church, State, and the Birth of Liberty* (New York: Viking Penguin, 2012), 251.

13 "William and Mary Barrett Dyer: Mary Dyer's 'monster,'" 24 May 2013, <http://marybarrettdyer.blogspot.com/2011/09/mary-dyers-monster.html>.

14 "William and Mary Barrett Dyer: Mary Dyer's 'monster.'"

15 "A Brief History of Anne M. Hutchinson," 20 September 2013, <http://annehutchinson.org/brief-history.html>.

16 Edward T. James, Janet Wilson James, and Paul S. Boyer, eds., *Notable American Women 1607–1950: A Biographical Dictionary*, Volume I, A–F (Cambridge, MA: The Belknap Press of Harvard University Press, 1971), 536.

17 Plimpton 137.

18 Plimpton 175.

19 Benjamin F. Thompson, *The History of Long Island From Its Discovery and Settlement, To The*

Present Time With Important and Interesting Matters; Including Notices of Numerous Individuals and Families; Also a Particular Account of The Different Churches and Ministers, Vol. II (New York: Gould, Banks & Co., 1843), 286–287.

[20] "Religious Freedom: The Trial of Anne Hutchinson," 2 August 2010, <http://pbskids.org/wayback/civilrights/features_hutchinson.html>.

[21] "Mass Moments: Quakers Outlawed in Plymouth Dec. 3 1658."

[22] Plimpton 155.

[23] Plimpton 156.

[24] Plimpton 162.

[25] Plimpton 164.

[26] Plimpton 165.

[27] James, James, and Boyer, 536.

[28] Plimpton 172.

[29] Plimpton 185.

[30] Laurence Barber, "Early Cape Quakers," 20 February 2013, <http://www.capecodquakers.org/earlyquakers.html>.

[31] James, James, and Boyer, 536.

[32] James, James, and Boyer, 537.

[33] "Mary Dyer," 18 February 2012, <http://www.nwhm.org/education-resources/biography/biographies/mary-dyer>.

[34] Plimpton 178.

[35] Christy K. Robinson, "Grandparents-in-law: The Quaker Connection," 21 February 2013, <http://marybarrettdyer.blogspot.com/2012/06/grandparents-in-law-quaker-connection.html>.

[36] Robinson.

[37] Col. Charles H. Weygant (compiler), *The Hull Family in America* (USA: Hull Family Association, 1913), 251.

[38] Weygant 260.

[39] Robinson.

CHAPTER FIVE The Flushing Remonstrance

[1] *A Memorial of John, Henry, and Richard Townsend, and Their Descendants* (New York: W. A. Townsend, 1865), 81.

[2] Thompson 294.

[3] Allison Putala, the Director of the Townsend Society of America, email, 13 March 2013.

4   *A Memorial* 211.

5   Anderson 438.

6   Anderson 438.

7   Anderson 438.

8   Anderson 438–439.

9   *A Memorial* 82.

10 "Kingston: Discover 300 Years of New York History," 12 March 2013,
    <http://www.nps.gov/nr/travel/kingston/colonization.htm>.

11 *A Memorial* 82.

12 *A Memorial* 82.

13 *A Memorial* 82.

14 New Netherland Institute: Exploring America's Dutch Heritage, "A Tour of New
    Netherland: Fort Amsterdam," 16 March 2013,
    <http://www.newnetherlandinstitute.org/history-and-heritage/digital-
    exhibitions/a-tour-of-new-netherland/manhattan/fort-amsterdam>.

15 Landmarks Preservation Commission, "Development of Jamaica," 12 March 2013,
    <http://www.nyc.gov/html/lpc/downloads/pdf/reports/2394.pdf>.

16 Thompson 288.

17 "Conventicles," 16 March 2013,
    <http://dictionary.reference.com/browse/conventicles>.

18 McCloud/Colgan Genealogy (unpublished family record), "Index:
    Townsend/Coles-Henry Townsend I and Anne Coles," cited by permission from
    Mrs. M. Parry

19 Thompson 290.

20 *A Memorial* 81.

21 *A Memorial* 83.

22 "Document: The Flushing Remonstrance, 1657," Dutch New York Rediscover 400
    Years of History, 20 November 2012,
    <http://www.thirteen.org/dutchny/interactives/document-the-flushing-
    remonstrance/12/#.UKw3-O0Y5UQ>.

23 "Remonstrance," 20 November 2012, <http://www.merriam-
    webster.com/dictionary/remonstrance>.

24 "Precursor of the Constitution Goes on Display in Queens," 20 November 2012,
    <http://www.nytimes.com/2007/12/05/nyregion/05remonstrance.html?_r=0>.

25 "Precursor of the Constitution."

26 "350ᵗʰ Anniversary of the Flushing Remonstrance: 1657-2007, A celebration of a document and the principles it embodies," 20 November 2012, <http://www.queensbp.org/remonstrance/index.html#notes>.

27 "350ᵗʰ Anniversary."

28 "350ᵗʰ Anniversary."

29 "Precursor of the Constitution."

30 *A Memorial* 83.

31 Thompson 291.

CHAPTER SIX The Pequot War

1 "Pequot Indian History," Native Americans: Pequot, 20 September 2013, <http://www.native-americans-of-the-southwest.info/pequots.htm>.

2 "1637-THE PEQUOT WAR," Society of Colonial Wars in the State of Connecticut, 30 November 2011, <http://www.colonialwarsct.org/1637.htm>.

3 *Mystic Voices: The Story of the Pequot War*. Dir. Guy Perrotta. Dir. Charles Clemmons. 2004. Mystic Voices LLC, 12 August 2004. DVD.

4 "History of Old Saybrook," 17 March 2013, <http://www.oldsaybrookct.org/Pages/OldSaybrookCT_About/living_history>.

5 "Lion Gardiner" interpretive marker, Fort Saybrook Monument Park, Old Saybrook, CT.

6 Charles Orr, *History of the Pequot War: The Contemporary Accounts of Mason, Underhill, Vincent and Gardener, Reprinted from the Collections of the Massachusetts Historical Society* (Cleveland, Ohio: The Helman-Taylor Company, 1897), 127.

7 "Welcome To Fort Saybrook" interpretive marker, Fort Saybrook Monument Park, Old Saybrook, CT.

8 Cypress Cemetery Saybrook Point, Old Saybrook, CT, 17 March 2013, <http://www.cypresscemeteryosct.org/saybrookfortruins.html>.

9 Richard Radune, "Thomas Stanton History," 30 November 2011, <http://stantonsociety.org/tshistory.html>.

10 John Mason, *A Brief History of the Pequot War*, (Bedford, MA: Applewood Books, [originally published in 1736]), 108.

CHAPTER SEVEN King Philip's War

1 John Gorham Palfrey, *History of New England*, Vol. I (Boston, MA: Little, Brown, and Company, 1858), 467.

2 Edward Wagenknecht, *A Pictorial History of New England* (New York: Crown Publishers, Inc., 1976), 43.

[3] Wagenknecht 296.

[4] Eric B. Schultz and Michael J. Tougias, *King Philip's War: The History and Legacy of America's Forgotten Conflict* (Woodstock, VT: The Countryman Press, 1999), 4–5.

[5] Duane Hamilton Hurd, ed., *The History of New London Country, Connecticut with Biographical Sketches of Many of Its Pioneers and Prominent Men* (Philadelphia: J. W. Lewis & Co, 1882), 620.

[6] The Denison Homestead, 19 March 2013, <http://denisonhomestead.org/venture-smith-and-the-denison-connection/archaeological-dig-for-the-palisades>.

[7] "About The Homestead," 19 March 2013, <http://denisonhomestead.org/denison-homestead/about>.

[8] Stonington Historical Society, *Stonington Graveyards: A Guide* (Stonington, CT: Stonington Historical Society, 1980), 11.

[9] William Richard Cutter, *New England Families, Genealogical and Memorial: A Record of the Achievements of Her People in the Making of Commonwealths and the Founding of a Nation*, Vol. II (New York: Lewis Historical Publishing Company, 1913), 861.

[10] Cutter 861.

[11] Cutter 861.

[12] George W. Ellis and John E. Morris, *King Philip's War; based on the Archives and Records of Massachusetts, Plymouth, Rhode Island and Connecticut, and Contemporary Letters and Accounts, with Biographical and Topographical Notes* (New York: The Grafton Press, 1906), 204–05.

[13] "King Philip's War and The "Sudbury Fight," A Brief History of the Town of Sudbury, MA, USA, 1 December 2011, <http://www.sudbury.ma.us/departments/seniorcenter/services/custom/hal/kpwar.htm>.

CHAPTER EIGHT Fighting for the Fort: The Grisly History of Fort Griswold

[1] "Fort Griswold Day: 230th Anniversary of Groton Battle a Huge Success." *The Acorn* (newsletter of the Ledyard Historical Society), Vol. 7.3 (Dec. 2011): 3.

[2] "The Battle of Groton Heights," Fort Griswold Home Page, 24 October 2012, <http://www.revwar.com/ftgriswold>.

[3] "Battle of Groton Heights," 24 October 2012, <http://www.battleofgrotonheights.com/Battle_of_Groton_Heights.html>.

[4] "Battle of Groton Heights."

[5] William W. Harris, *The Battle of Groton Heights: A Collection of Narratives, Official Reports, Records, etc., of the Storming of Fort Griswold, The Massacre of its Garrison, and the Burning of New London by British Troops under the Command of Brig.-Gen. Benedict Arnold, on the Sixth of September, 1781* (New London, CT: Charles Allyn, 1882), 262–63.

6   Harris 262–63.

7   "The Ebenezer Avery House," Joe Lantiere, ed., 31 December 2011,
    <http://www.averymemorialassociation.com/ebavery.htm>.

8   Joshua Hempstead, *The Diary of Joshua Hempstead: A Daily Record of Life in Colonial New
    London, Connecticut 1711-1758 with an account of an overland journey the writer made to
    Maryland and back in 1749* (New London, CT: New London County Historical
    Society, Inc., 1999), 527.

9   Hempstead 528.

10 Kathleen Greenhalgh, *A History of Old Mystic 1600–1999* (United States of America:
    Published by Kathleen Greenhalgh, 1999), 73.

11 Greenhalgh 73.

CHAPTER NINE Revolutionary Love

1   "The Battle of White Plains," 30 March 2013,
    <http://www.britishbattles.com/white-plains.htm>.

2   "The Battle of White Plains."

3   "The Battle of White Plains."

4   Kennedy Hickman, "American Revolution: Battle of White Plains," 30 March 2013,
    <http://militaryhistory.about.com/od/americanrevolution/p/whiteplains.htm?vm=
    r>.

5   "The Battle of White Plains," 30 March 2013,
    <http://www.britishbattles.com/white-plains.htm>.

6   "The Battle of White Plains," 30 March 2013,
    <http://theamericanrevolution.org/battledetail.aspx?battle=11>.

7   "Military Medicine During The Revolutionary War," 30 March 2013,
    <http://www.au.af.mil/au/awc/awcgate/milmedhist/chapter2.htm>.

8   Walter Frederic Brooks, *History Of The Fanning Family: A Genealogical Record to 1900 of
    The Descendants of Edmund Fanning, The Emigrant Ancestor in America, who settled in Connecticut
    in 1653* (Worcester, MA: privately printed, 1905), 199.

9   Brooks 200.

10 Brooks 147.

11 "Groton-Ledyard Marriages," 31 March 2013,
    <http://homepage.ct.metrocast.net/~kamaba/NewLondonCo/grotonmarriages.
    htm>.

12 "Groton-Ledyard Marriages."

13 Janice Wightman Bell and Shelia Anyan Godino, eds., *Historic Ledyard*, Vol. III
    (Norwich, CT: Franklin Impressions, Inc., 1998), 221.

14 Entry from record of marriages and births recorded by William Williams, Justice of the Peace, William Williams Family Collection, Ledyard Historical Society, Ledyard, Connecticut.

15 Carolyn Smith and Helen Vergason, *September 6, 1781: North Groton's Story* (New London, CT: New London Printers, Inc., 1981), 30.

CHAPTER TEN The War of 1812

1 James Tertius De Kay, *The Battle of Stonington: Torpedoes, Submarines, and Rockets in the War of 1812* (Hyannis, MA: Parnassus Imprints, 1990), 1.

2 Benson J. Lossing, *The Pictorial Field-Book of the War of 1812 or, Illustrations, By Pen and Pencil, of the History, Biography, Scenery, Relics, and Traditions of the Last War For American Independence*, Vol. 2 (Gretna, LA: Pelican Publishing Company, 2001), 893.

3 Lossing 893.

4 Lossing 893.

5 Barbara Trueblood Abbott, *Matilda's Letters* (Old Greenwich, CT: Privately Printed by Barbara Trueblood Abbott, 1974), 9.

6 Abbott 11.

7 Abbott 11–12.

CHAPTER ELEVEN Cider Hill Farm Homecoming

1 Connecticut Poorhouse History, "Special Report: Paupers in Almshouses, 1904," 4 April 2013,
    <http://www.poorhousestory.com/poorhouses_in_connecticut.htm>.

2 "Letter To Doctor Marshall written by Mrs. Dorothy Gray Brown, August 30, 1972," William Williams Family Collection, Ledyard Historical Society, Ledyard, CT.

3 "Aura of Misfortune Surrounding Old Farm Replaced By Feelings of Warmth and Love," 30 October 1978, newspaper article in the William Williams Family Collection, Ledyard Historical Society, Ledyard, CT.

4 "Aura of Misfortune."

5 "Aura of Misfortune."

6 "About Your Farmers," 7 April 2013, <http://townfarmorganic.com/about>.

7 "Commander's Call," Ledyard VFW Post 4608, 28 July 2010,
    <http://orgsites.com/ct/vfwpost4608>.

CHAPTER TWELVE Pictures Are Worth a Thousand Words

No endnotes

CHAPTER THIRTEEN Slavery in Connecticut

1   Douglas Harper, "Slavery in the North," 18 November 2011,
    <http://www.slavenorth.com/index.html>.

2   Douglas Harper, "Slavery in Connecticut," 22 July 2013,
    <http://www.slavenorth.com/connecticut.htm>.

3   "Slavery in Connecticut."

4   John Wood Sweet, "Venture Smith, from Slavery to Freedom," 22 July 2013,
    <http://connecticuthistory.org/venture-smith-from-slavery-to-freedom>.

5   "Venture Smith."

6   "Slavery in Connecticut."

7   Richard Anson Wheeler, *History of the Town of Stonington, County of New London,
    Connecticut, From Its Settlement in 1649 to 1900 with a Genealogical Register of Stonington Families*
    (New London, Connecticut: Press of the Day Publishing Company, 1900), 640.

8   Wheeler 731.

9   Wheeler 734.

10 Wheeler 730.

11 Wheeler 731.

12 Wheeler 731.

13 "History of Cider Hill Farm (Town Farm)," William Williams Family Collection,
    Ledyard Historical Society, Ledyard, CT, 1.

CHAPTER FOURTEEN The Stanton-Davis Homestead:
Where Indian Law, English Law, and Slavery Intersected

1   "Facts and Details About The Homestead," Stanton-Davis Homestead Museum,
    17 September 2010, <http://stantondavishomestead.org/homestead.html>.

2   "Denison Redding Apple Comes Home," Denison Homestead Newsletter,
    Fall/Winter 2010, No. 139, 3.

3   John Lawrence Davis, *The Davis Homestead: A Farm Since 1680 in Lower Pawcatuck,
    Connecticut* (Stonington, CT: The Stonington Historical Society, 2007), 20.

4   "Facts and Details About The Homestead," Stanton-Davis Homestead Museum,
    17 September 2010, <http://stantondavishomestead.org/homestead.html>.

5   Evans, "Denison Redding Apple Comes Home."

6   "The Stanton-Davis Homestead Museum," 17 September 2010,
    <http://stantondavishomestead.org/homestead.html>.

CHAPTER FIFTEEN Colonial Chroniclers

1   "First Parish History," 16 April 2013,
    <http://www.firstparishcambridge.org/?q=FirstParishHistory>.

2   "The History of Cambridge: Mr. Shepard," 16 April 2013,
    <http://www.harvardsquarelibrary.org/chistory/section63shepard.htm>.

CHAPTER SIXTEEN From Pulpit to Paper: Reverend Thomas Shepard and His Journal

1   Michael McGiffert, ed., *God's Plot: Puritan Spirituality in Thomas Shepard's Cambridge*
    (Amherst, MA: University of Massachusetts Press, 1994), 3.

2   Thomas Shepard, *The Sincere Convert and The Sound Believer: With a Memoir of His Life and
    Character*, lithographed from the 1853 edition published by the Boston Doctrinal
    Tract and Book Society, (Morgan, PA: Soli Deo Gloria Publications, 1999), xii.

3   Shepard xxii.

4   "Hudson-Mohawk Genealogical and Family Memoirs: Shepard," 16 April 2013,
    <http://schenectadyhistory.org/families/hmgfm/shepard.html>.

5   McGiffert 31.

6   McGiffert cli.

7   Thomas Shepard and John A. Albro, D.D., *The Works of Thomas Shepard, First Pastor of
    the First Church, Cambridge, Mass: With a Memoir of His Life and Character* (Memphis, TN:
    General Books, 2010), 88.

8   Shepard xii.

9   Randall C. Gleason, "Thomas Shepard: The Man Who Inspired Jonathan
    Edwards," 17 April 2013, <https://www.lifeaction.org/revival-resources/heart-
    cry-journal/issue-47/thomas-shepard-man-who-inspired-jonathan-edwards>.

10 Shepard cli-clii.

CHAPTER SEVENTEEN New London's Native Son: Joshua Hempstead and His Diary

1   Frances Manwaring Caulkins, *History of New London, Connecticut From The First Survey of
    the Coast in 1612 to 1852* (New London, CT: Published by the author, 1852), 273.

2   Hempstead iv.

3   "The Joshua Hempstead Diary," 18 April 2013,
    <http://newlondongazette.com/hempintr.html>.

4 Hempstead iii.

5 Hempstead 57.

6 Hempstead 57–58.

7 Hempstead 209.

8 "Historic Sites of New London, Connecticut," New London Gazette, 4 July 2011, <http://newlondongazette.com/histrc.html>.

9 Kathleen Edgecomb, "Long-lost diary pages coming home to New London," Day Newspaper, 1 June 2013, <http://www.theday.com/article/20110726/NWS01/307269958/1017>.

10 "Guide To First Period Architecture in the Essex National Heritage Area," Essex National Heritage Area, 17 November 2012, <http://www.essexheritage.org/firstperiod>.

11 "Connecticut Landmarks-Hempsted Houses," Connecticut Landmarks, 1 April 2011, <http://www.ctlandmarks.org/index.php?page=hempsted-houses>.

12 "Connecticut Landmarks-Hempsted Houses."

CHAPTER EIGHTEEN Stonington Stories: Thomas Minor and His Diary

1 "Old Mystic Cemetery Has Rare Wolf Stones," 18 April 2013, <http://www.archaeologydaily.com/news/201011015433/Old-Mystic-Cemetery-Has-Rare-Wolf-Stones.html>.

2 "Old Mystic Cemetery."

3 Thomas Minor, The Diary of Thomas Minor, Stonington, Connecticut: 1653-1684 ([no town given] US: Kessinger Publishing Legacy Reprints, no date of publication), 4.

4 Sidney H. Miner and George D. Stanton, Jr., eds., The Diary of Thomas Minor, Stonington, Connecticut: 1653 to 1684, (New London: CT: Press of the Day Publishing Company, 1899), 192.

5 Miner and Stanton 132–133.

CHAPTER NINETEEN As One Journey Ends, Others Begin

No endnotes

Bibliography

References to Internet websites (URLs) were correct at the time this book was written. The author is not responsible for URLs which may have been changed or expired.

Abbott, Barbara Trueblood. *Matilda's Letters*. Old Greenwich, CT: Privately printed by Barbara Trueblood Abbott, 1974.

"A Brief History of Anne M. Hutchinson." The Friends of Anne Hutchinson. http://annehutchinson.org/brief-history.html.

"Alden's Duxbury Houses: John Alden & Priscilla Mullins Biography." Alden Kindred of America. www.alden.org/our_family/aldenbiography.htm#Children.

"Alden House Virtual Tour: The Great Room." Alden House Historic Site. www.alden.org/Virtual%20Tour/tour.htm.

Anderson, Robert Charles. *The Great Migration Begins: Immigrants to New England 1620–1633*, Volume I, A–F. Boston: New England Historic Genealogical Society, 1995.

"Anne Hutchinson and the Antinomian Controversy." http://faculty.samford.edu/~whbunch/Case%202.pdf.

"Anne Hutchinson and John Wheelwright." www.americanancestors.org/great-migration-newsletter-anne-hutchinson.

A Memorial of John, Henry, and Richard Townsend, and Their Descendants. New York: W. A. Townsend, 1865.

Barber, Laurence. "Early Cape Quakers." Sandwich Monthly Meeting. www.capecodquakers.org/earlyquakers.html.

Barry, John M. *Roger Williams and The Creation of the American Soul: Church, State, and the Birth of Liberty*. New York: Viking Penguin, 2012.

"Battle of Groton Heights." www.battleofgrotonheights.com/Battle_of_Groton_Heights.html.

Bell, Janice Wightman and Shelia Anyan Godino, eds., *Historic Ledyard*, Vol. III. Norwich, CT: Franklin Impressions, Inc., 1998.

"Biography of Walter Palmer." Walter Palmer Society. http://walterpalmer.com/Walter_Palmer_Bio.htm.

Brooks, Walter Frederic. *History Of The Fanning Family: A Genealogical Record to 1900 of The Descendants of Edmund Fanning, The Emigrant Ancestor in America, who settled in Connecticut in 1653.* Worcester, MA: privately printed, 1905.

Caulkins, Frances Manwaring. *The History of New London, Connecticut From The First Survey of the Coast in 1612 to 1852.* New London: CT, published by the author, 1852.

Cutter, William Richard. *New England Families, Genealogical and Memorial: A Record of the Achievements of Her People in the Making of Commonwealths and the Founding of a Nation,* Vol. II. New York: Lewis Historical Publishing Company, 1913.

Davis, John Lawrence. *The Davis Homestead: A Farm Since 1680 in Lower Pawcatuck, Connecticut.* Stonington, CT: The Stonington Historical Society, 2007.

De Kay, James Tertius. *The Battle of Stonington: Torpedoes, Submarines, and Rockets in the War of 1812.* Hyannis, MA: Parnassus Imprints, 1990.

"Document: The Flushing Remonstrance, 1657." Dutch New York Rediscover 400 Years of History. www.thirteen.org/dutchny/interactives/document-the-flushing-remonstrance/12/#.UKw3-O0Y5UQ.

"Dutch Colonies." Kingston: Discover 300 Years of New York History. www.nps.gov/nr/travel/kingston/colonization.htm.

Ellis, George W., and John E. Morris, *King Philip's War; based on the Archives and Records of Massachusetts, Plymouth, Rhode Island and Connecticut, and Contemporary Letters and Accounts, with Biographical and Topographical Notes.* New York: The Grafton Press, 1906.

"Five Generations Project." Alden Kindred of America. www.alden.org/genealogy/documents/five-gen1.html#HISTORY.

"Fort Amsterdam." New Netherland Institute: Exploring America's Dutch Heritage. www.newnetherlandinstitute.org/history-and-heritage/digital-exhibitions/a-tour-of-new-netherland/manhattan/fort-amsterdam.

"Fort Griswold Day: 230th Anniversary of Groton Battle a Huge Success." *The Acorn* (newsletter of the Ledyard Historical Society), Vol. 7.3, Dec. 2011.

Frost, Josephine C., ed., *Underhill Genealogy,* Vol. I. Privately published by Myron C. Taylor, 1932.

Goodman, Mary Virginia and Joe Lantiere, ed. "The Ebenezer Avery House." www.averymemorialassociation.com/ebavery.htm.

Greenhalgh, Kathleen. *A History of Old Mystic 1600–1999.* United States of America: Published by Kathleen Greenhalgh, 1999.

"Groton-Ledyard Marriages."
http://homepage.ct.metrocast.net/~kamaba/NewLondonCo/grotonmarriages.htm.

Harper, Douglas. "Slavery in the North." www.slavenorth.com/index.html.

Harris, William W. *The Battle of Groton Heights: A Collection of Narratives, Official Reports, Records, etc., of the Storming of Fort Griswold, The Massacre of its Garrison, and the Burning of New London by British Troops under the Command of Brig.-Gen. Benedict Arnold, on the Sixth of September, 1781*. New London, CT: Charles Allyn, 1882.

Hempstead, Joshua. *The Diary of Joshua Hempstead: A Daily Record of Life in Colonial New London, Connecticut 1711-1758 with an account of an overland journey the writer made to Maryland and back in 1749*. New London, CT: New London County Historical Society, Inc., 1999.

Hickman, Kennedy. "American Revolution: Battle of White Plains."
http://militaryhistory.about.com/od/americanrevolution/p/whiteplains.htm?vm=r.

Hurd, Duane Hamilton, ed., *The History of New London Country, Connecticut with Biographical Sketches of Many of Its Pioneers and Prominent Men*. Philadelphia: J. W. Lewis & Co, 1882.

James, Edward T., Janet Wilson James, and Paul S. Boyer, eds., *Notable American Women 1607–1950: A Biographical Dictionary*, Volume I, A–F. Cambridge, Massachusetts: The Belknap Press of Harvard University Press, 1971.

"King Philip's War and The "Sudbury Fight." A Brief History of the Town of Sudbury, MA, USA.
www.sudbury.ma.us/departments/seniorcenter/services/custom/hal/kpwar.htm.

Lossing, Benson J. *The Pictorial Field-Book of the War of 1812 or, Illustrations, By Pen and Pencil, of the History, Biography, Scenery, Relics, and Traditions of the Last War For American Independence*, Vol. 2. Gretna, LA: Pelican Publishing Company, 2001.

Marchand, Roland. "The Antinomian Controversy (University)." The History Project-University of California, Davis.
http://historyproject.ucdavis.edu/lessons/view_lesson.php?id=8.

Mason, John. *A Brief History of the Pequot War*. Bedford, MA: Applewood Books, [originally published in 1736].

Michael McGiffert, ed., *God's Plot: Puritan Spirituality in Thomas Shepard's Cambridge*. Amherst, MA: University of Massachusetts Press, 1994.

McManus, Edgar J. *Law and Liberty in Early New England: Criminal Justice and Due Process, 1620–1692*. Amherst, MA: University of Massachusetts Press, 1993.

Miner, Sidney H. and George D. Stanton, Jr., eds., *The Diary of Thomas Minor, Stonington,*

Connecticut: 1653 to 1684. New London: CT: Press of the Day Publishing Company, 1899.

Mystic Voices: The Story of the Pequot War. Dir. Guy Perrotta. Dir. Charles Clemmons. 2004. Mystic Voices LLC, 12 August 2004. DVD.

Nadler, Matthew. "Vermont man learns about his ancestors in Duxbury." Wicked Local Duxbury. www.wickedlocal.com/duxbury/features/x1696237692/Vermont-man-learns-about-his-ancestors-in-Duxbury?zc_p=0#axzz2UW6hkxfw.

Palfrey, John Gorham. *History of New England*, Vol. I. Boston, MA: Little, Brown, and Company, 1858.

Plimpton, Ruth Talbot. *Mary Dyer: Biography of a Rebel Quaker*. Boston, MA: Branden Publishing Company, Inc., 1994.

Orr, Charles. *History of the Pequot War: The Contemporary Accounts of Mason, Underhill, Vincent and Gardener, Reprinted from the Collections of the Massachusetts Historical Society*. Cleveland, Ohio: The Helman-Taylor Company, 1897.

Radune, Richard. "Thomas Stanton History." The Thomas Stanton Society. http://stantonsociety.org/tshistory.html.

Robinson, Christy K. "William and Mary Barrett Dyer: Mary Dyer's 'monster.'" http://marybarrettdyer.blogspot.com/2011/09/mary-dyers-monster.html.

————. "Grandparents-in-law: The Quaker Connection." http://marybarrettdyer.blogspot.com/2012/06/grandparents-in-law-quaker-connection.html.

Schultz, Eric B., and Michael J. Tougias. *King Philip's War: The History and Legacy of America's Forgotten Conflict*. Woodstock, VT: The Countryman Press, 1999.

Shepard, Thomas. *The Sincere Convert and The Sound Believer: With a Memoir of His Life and Character*, lithographed from the 1853 edition published by the Boston Doctrinal Tract and Book Society. Morgan, PA: Soli Deo Gloria Publications, 1999.

Shepard, Thomas and John A. Albro, D.D., *The Works of Thomas Shepard, First Pastor of the First Church, Cambridge, Mass: With a Memoir of His Life and Character*. Memphis, TN: General Books, 2010.

Smith, Carolyn and Helen Vergason. *September 6, 1781: North Groton's Story*. New London, CT: New London Printers, Inc., 1981.

"Special Report: Paupers in Almshouses, 1904." Connecticut Poorhouse History. www.poorhousestory.com/poorhouses_in_connecticut.htm.

Stonington Historical Society. *Stonington Graveyards: A Guide.* Stonington, CT: Stonington Historical Society, 1980.

"The Freemen of the Massachusetts Bay Colony 1630–1636." The Winthrop Society. www.winthropsociety.com/doc_freemen.php.

"The Great Migration, A Survey of New England: 1620-1640." The Great Migration Study Project. www.greatmigration.org.

Thompson, Benjamin F. *The History of Long Island From Its Discovery and Settlement, To The Present Time With Important and Interesting Matters; Including Notices of Numerous Individuals and Families; Also a Particular Account of The Different Churches and Ministers*, Vol. II. New York: Gould, Banks & Co., 1843.

Wagenknecht, Edward. *A Pictorial History of New England.* New York: Crown Publishers, Inc., 1976.

Weygant, Col. Charles H. *The Hull Family in America.* United States: Hull Family Association, 1913.

Wheeler, Richard Anson. *History of the Town of Stonington, County of New London, Connecticut, From Its Settlement in 1649-1900 with a Genealogical Register of Stonington Families.* New London, CT: Press of the Day Publishing Company, 1900.

Woodworth-Barnes, Esther Littleford, and Alicia Crane Williams, ed., *Mayflower Families Through Five Generations: Descendants of the Pilgrims Who Landed at Plymouth, Mass.*, December 1620, Family of John Alden, Vol. 16. 1. Plymouth, MA: General Society of *Mayflower* Descendants, 1999.

"1637-THE PEQUOT WAR." Society of Colonial Wars in the State of Connecticut. www.colonialwarsct.org/1637.htm.

Index

(Illustrations are indicated by italic numerals)

Acknowledgements

In the eighteen years between the conception of this book and its materialization there have been many individuals who helped bring it to life. I attended the Brooks Middle School in Lincoln, Massachusetts where Mr. Ben Potter and Mrs. Jane Benes who were 8th grade teachers both nurtured my passion for history and writing. I am grateful to these teachers and many others in the Lincoln Public School system who inspired me to do what I love-write and research history.

The research for this book started in my 8th grade history class. My first thank-you goes to Ben Potter for setting me on the path to writing this book and for inspiring me to ask questions of my grandparents and relatives starting in 1994. Another special thanks goes to my 8th grade classmate and friend Elizabeth "Liz" Mygatt who shared that her ancestor Joseph Mygatt had his name listed on the Founders of Hartford Monument in Hartford, Connecticut. Liz's mention of her ancestor made me wish I too had an ancestor who was a founder of Hartford. I was truly surprised to find that I had two ancestors-Thomas Lord and his son-in-law Thomas Stanton whose names are also listed on the Founders of Hartford Monument in the Ancient Burying Ground in Hartford, Connecticut.

Huge thanks go out to Derek Krein, Joe Sheppard, Rob Moore, Tony Hawgood, John Curran, and Chris Margraf who were amazing teachers and mentors during my time as a high school student at Lawrence Academy in Groton, Massachusetts. Mr. Sheppard deserves an extra special thank-you for sticking with me during my college application process. He knew long before I did that Denison University was going to be the perfect college for me to attend. He was right all along.

Dr. Mitchell Snay, Dr. Amy Gordon, and Dr. Michael Gordon were college professors and mentors for me at Denison University. They all inspired me to do thorough historical research and above all to love the research process. I had no idea while visiting their offices in Fellow Hall that my love for English history would give way to an incredible passion for colonial American history. I would not be the researcher and independent scholar I am today without all of their patience, guidance, and feedback throughout my four years at Denison.

Encouragement, advice, and support for this book has come from teachers, professors, friends, and family. I dearly wish that I could share the first copies of this book with my grandparents Faith and Jim, my brother Nick, and Corinne Breed. My grandparents did an amazing job of sharing family information and memories with me during the Thanksgiving of 1994 and throughout 1995. The information they were able to share made this book possible. I never expected to find out so much about Williams ancestors because it was such a common last name. Corinne Breed forever changed my life when she opened her door to me during Halloween weekend of 2009. I contacted her after finding a picture of her with her husband labeled "Mystic cousins on their wedding anniversary" from 1968. Corinne made so much of this book possible by connecting my mother and I with Delight Wolfe and Betty Tylaska. Delight, Betty, and Corinne knew more about my ancestors and our extended family tree in Connecticut than I ever could have imagined. Delight and Betty have both helped enormously with the task of piecing together three and half centuries of family history. Betty is responsible for sending me to the Hempsted Houses in New London and Delight inspired my visit to Clermont, Iowa and Montauk.

Pam Fenn's bookshop The Barrow Bookstore in Concord, Massachusetts has been a source of historical materials since the day I sat down to write this book. The discovery made one day in the bookshop that Pam and I share Minor and Palmer family heritage made for a delightful surprise!

Fred and Evelyn Burdick also deserve special thank-yous for helping me with research in the greater Stonington area. Fred helped me locate family burying grounds and he helped me piece together huge pieces of my family tree in the greater Mystic area.

My meeting with Janice Bell at the Ledyard Historical Society in August 2000 led to the revelation that my Williams ancestors owned slaves. This was the first time I had heard of slavery in New England and a direct ancestral connection to slavery. Later Chandler B. Saint and John "Whit" Davis were instrumental in sharing information about slavery in the North, slave-owning Stantons and Denisons, their lives, and the homes they lived in. Learning from each of them about Venture Smith forever changed my views of New England history.

Phyllis J. Crick and her husband Harvey Crick in Darke County, Ohio helped me uncover my Kiester and Bashore roots. Without them, my Palatine German roots would have remained a secret. Doug and Margie Appelman shared Williams family history in Iowa and helped me piece together my family's 19th Century history. Lois Macy was extremely helpful when it came to researching my Robert Williams lineage. Wade Schott and his colleagues at Montauk Historic Site brought the lives of the Larrabee family vividly to life and helped me access the rich historical photographic archives there. Matilda and Bob Rupp and Molly and Dick Parry were all wonderfully generous during my visit to Minneapolis in establishing family links down the generations and showing me family crests, heirlooms, and sharing family stories. Joyce Okey aided me in compiling Appelman family information and she too gets huge thank-yous for all of the help she provided. Thank-yous to Louisa Alger Watrous who helped this book become a reality. Edward Baker, Sally Ryan, and Barbara Nagy all assisted me when it came to researching my Hempstead family roots. John Adams helped me with King Philip's War research and inspired me to visit Smith's Castle in Wickford, Rhode Island to learn about the Great Swamp Fight of 1675. John Banks provided new information on Hiram Appleman, his life, and experiences during The Battle of Antietam.

Important primary research for this book came from institutions including the New England Historic Genealogical Society, Connecticut Historical Society, Connecticut State Library, Iowa Genealogical Society, Ohio Historical Society, Mystic River Historical Society, Ledyard Historical Society, The Mayflower Society, The Alden Kindred of America, Ancient & Honorable Artillery Company of Massachusetts, Clermont Historical Society, The Ancient Burying Ground Association, Dayton History, Indian and Colonial Research Center, The Thomas Minor Society, The Thomas Stanton Society, The Denison Homestead, The New London County Historical Society, The Newport Historical Society, The Townsend Society, The Denison Society, The Winthrop Society, The Underhill Society of America, and the achives of the Honourable Artillery Company.

This book would not be what it is today without the hard work of my talented editor Susan Schmidt. She was able to see the potential of this narrative in its early days and she helped me polish its rough edges. Her detailed and thought provoking edits made me reimagine the stories I was telling and the stories came to life.

I am grateful for all of the friends and family members who supported me as the narrative took shape and who listened to the stories of my genealogical and historical adventures "in the field." Patrick Hoy and Julian Radcliffe were there at the dinner in London when the book's title became official and their unwavering support means the world to me. There have many wonderful friends who encouraged me to go out "into the field" to experience history. When that meant getting my boots on and grabbing tick spray for the deep grass and heavily wooded areas they motivated me to do so. To these friends, I am equally indebted.

Special thanks to those fellow writers who took the time to assure me this book would one day be published and to Lily Taylor, who is a friend, editor, and an inspiration.

Trish LaPointe did a superb job as the graphic designer given the task of bringing this book to life via page and picture layout. Andrew German did a great job creating the index for the book. The indexing work was challenging as many of my ancestors had the same first and last names and were alive at the same time. He did a thoughtful and thorough job creating an index that incorporated centuries worth of material. Emily Mygatt Lee the talented photographer and owner of Roxbury Photography took my author photo.

Above all, this book was made possible by the unconditional love, support, and guidance of my parents Dan and Katherine and my brother Nick. My family continues to inspire me to take a path less traveled by and to do work that I love each and every day. In the spring of 2009 Nick gave me the ultimate birthday present-tickets to see The Killers perform at Mohegan Sun and my return to ancestral stomping grounds kicked started the writing of this book. Nick and I had a memorable time in June 2010 touring ancestral sites around Mystic and Stonington and I was so proud to show him our heritage. Mom, Dad, Nick-thank-you for helping me realize a dream I've had since I was fourteen.

Lastly, this book would not have ever been written if not for the extraordinary lives of my ancestors. This book is a tribute to the courageous men and women who shaped my family tree and who I am today.

About the Author

Katherine Dimancescu has been writing stories since she was a child. She has loved history, genealogy, and historical research since she was young. Writing and publishing this book has been a dream of hers since 1995. She received a BA in history from Denison University. She was awarded master's degrees in international relations from the University of Westminster, London, and the London School of Economics and Political Science. Prior to writing this book, she was a managing editor of international tax, law, and finance reports. She divides her time between Connecticut and Massachusetts.

NOTES

NOTES

Made in the USA
Middletown, DE
21 September 2015